Stuck

Stuck

How to WIN at Work by Understanding LOSS

Victoria Grady
Patrick McCreesh

Routledge
Taylor & Francis Group
A PRODUCTIVITY PRESS BOOK

First published 2022
by Routledge
605 Third Avenue, New York, NY 10158

and by Routledge
2 Park Square, Milton Park, Abingdon, Oxon, OX14 4RN

Routledge is an imprint of the Taylor & Francis Group, an informa business

ISBN: 978-0-367-74362-8 (hbk)
ISBN: 978-0-367-74361-1 (pbk)
ISBN: 978-1-00-315745-8 (ebk)

DOI: 10.4324/9781003157458

Typeset in Minion
by Newgen Publishing UK

From Victoria
For David, Kendall, Reagan

From Patrick
For Courtney, Lizzie, Rose, Bridget and Ginger

Contents

Preface

This is a book about the brain, the human experience, and how our life experiences shape our behavior at work. It's easy to say that we can divide work and life into two neat camps, but we come to work with the same brain we use in the rest of our lives. Our brain is formed by memory, emotion, and learning into a powerful force that makes us who we are as people. It helps us create powerful solutions for problem-solving and makes us resist even the simplest changes. This is when we get Stuck. When life's evolution makes it hard for us to move forward even though every rational piece of data says, "Just move on."

This book is a journey to understand why we get Stuck and how leaders and organizations can use research to guide themselves, their teams, and their organizations in a deeply human and more effective way. The journey of this book started 20 years ago. More precisely the research for this book started 20 years ago. However, that's not really where the journey started. Like everyone, our journey to understand the human experience started the day we were born. We both had challenges that led us to understand why people get Stuck. There is both a personal story that guided our interest and a professional story that led us to this book.

VICTORIA'S PERSONAL STORY OF BEING STUCK

I went to college and I did well. I got my master's degree and did okay. I got married after I finished my master's degree then moved to Europe. We were ticking the boxes. Getting the European Experience. I was teaching for University of Maryland's European Division and my husband was fulfilling his dream of practicing law with the 1st Infantry Division of the US Army – The Big Red One. We were experiencing cultural diversity, learning new languages, and traveling the world. The first year took us to eight different countries.

Then, after a very short honeymoon (or at least it seemed short), my husband received what would prove to be a terminal cancer diagnosis. My entire world came to a screeching halt. It came to a halt because every-thing I thought to be the next steps, the next piece in the puzzle, the next part of the journey of life as I expected it be…had suddenly stopped. It stopped because my husband had been diagnosed with terminal illness. In one brief conversation, I lost my connection to everything I thought to be true, secure, or stable. Everything changed.

The thought I struggled with the most, the thing that I kept thinking about was, "WOW – look how attached I was to my perception of what my life would (or could) be…what it would look like." Throughout my life I was completely attached to the concept that if you do X, Y, and Z, then of course A, B, and C are going to happen as a foregone conclusion. After my husband's initial diagnosis, I spent a great deal of time on self-reflection to better understand the role that my instinctual attachment to my pre-vious life had on my ability to pivot, shift, and move forward. I was initially paralyzed by the disruption. My mental model was thrown into total chaos, and it hindered my ability to engage when he needed me most. I was Stuck.

PATRICK'S PERSONAL STORY OF BEING STUCK

I have always been good at keeping important commitments. Especially commitments to the people who are close to me. My friend Joe was one of the people I most admired in the world. His carefree spirit was the personification of the duck – calm on the surface but paddling furiously underneath the water. Joe worked hard at everything and, to me, was the American Spirit. He grew up in Oklahoma, played high school football, had eclectic music taste, and loved the open road. He was insanely well-read and came to the University of Virginia to study English. He went on to work as a paralegal and, despite my best efforts to convince him otherwise, Joe decided to go to law school.

We were living in Washington, DC after college when I made a commitment to Joe. There was a last-minute surprise concert by Bob Dylan at the iconic 9:30 Club in DC. I got two tickets and Joe got zero. Of course, he was going to take the other ticket. But, I forgot about Courtney. A month prior to the tickets even going on sale, my old friend Courtney told me she would be visiting from New York the same night as the Dylan concert. I called her nervously two nights before her visit to explain why

I would now not be able to see her. I told her about the concert and she said, "I love Bob Dylan; that sounds great."

I then called Joe. I told him what happened and explained that I didn't know what to do. I even suggested perhaps that he and Courtney go to the show. His response, like the duck, was calm and direct, "She can go, but you have to marry her." She went to the show with me and we have been married for 15 years now. I take my commitments seriously.

Ok, I did not marry my wife because my friend told me to, but that night did become our first date thanks to Joe.

Over the next few years, Joe and I had a few adventures on the open road. We drove to Austin, TX from Washington, DC and back over two weeks in a search for the best BBQ. We made a few road trips for concerts. We got really into European soccer and recorded matches during the day to watch them after work. He was a groomsman in my wedding, and I helped him think about advancing his own romantic relationship. We also made long-term plans. I was going to pursue my Ph.D. and after he finished law school, plus working a few years in a big firm, he was going to write travel novels.

Two weeks after we celebrated my 30th birthday, Joe died in a Metro accident. I still don't know what happened. It was the middle of the World Cup and we were joking about the matches via text while I was in New Jersey visiting family. The loss was terrible. Our whole group of friends from college drove from DC to Oklahoma City for the funeral in what felt like an extended funeral processional.

A year after the accident, I decided to follow-through on another commitment I made to Joe. I enrolled to get my Ph.D. It wasn't solely because of Joe, but to this day I don't know how to separate the two things. I knew when he died that I couldn't say, "I will get to it later" anymore. I had to move on the important things right away. Joe became a symbol of a Carpe Diem spirit I think I always had, but somehow became intensified. It became intensified with a desire to complete things, to follow-through on commitments.

We had our second child the first semester of my Doctoral program and a third before I finished. I worked full-time in a consulting job and did classes at night, before moving into the dissertation. It was hard. It was harder for my wife. There were no more Dylan concerts. At the worst points, I constantly thought to myself, "Why am I doing this?" It seemed like I was not only focused on keeping commitments, but I was Stuck on my commitments. Why was I so Stuck on this idea of commitments? It seems deeply connected to Joe's memory. Joe became the reason to fulfill commitments that I make, simply because I am here, and I can. But why?

Our personal stories led us both to seek research on how people react to situations of loss and change. As Victoria mentions, we were also seeing it in our professional lives. Both of us were working with technology consulting engagements where we saw people continue to struggle with the adoption of new technology. Even when they understood exactly *what* the technology would do and even *why* they should use it, we would see them reject it completely. We both knew that something else was going on. And we had to understand what it was.

VICTORIA'S PROFESSIONAL INTEREST IN PEOPLE GETTING STUCK

Fifteen years ago, during my masters' degree graduate studies, I was employed as a senior manager in the software training industry. Daily, I found myself perplexed by the intensely emotional response of individual employees from all types of organizations when new technology was introduced. Later in my career, I witnessed a similar reaction from individual employees impacted by change in management, leadership, and business processes as well. People were reacting emotionally to change in almost any organizational context, but I could find no thread to understand the connection. To begin my investigation, I started taking notes and putting them in a folder under this title: "Notes on common responses in individuals to different types of organizational change and the difficulties these responses present."

These notes ended up spanning six years and two continents, with observations from the southern, eastern, and northeastern United States and central and southern Germany. I recorded my conversations with exasperated employees in geographically, demographically, and culturally distinct areas, and their reaction to change in technology, business processes, leadership, physical location, and structure. They all inadvertently identified an intense internal struggle in dealing with change. It wasn't that these individual employees were not good at change, or that they hated change, or that they were resistant to change, it was as if they were all dealing with an internal struggle that seemed inherent to the process of adjusting to change. And this internal struggle was not responding to external solutions. But why?

In 2001, I gained some additional insight into the answer, as I found myself sitting in an Individual and Group Dynamics course at The George Washington University. Dr. Jerry B. Harvey was presenting a new concept he termed the "anaclitic depression blues," and he was in full control of my attention. His topic came from a chapter in his recently published book, *How Come Every Time I Get Stabbed in the Back My Fingerprints Are on the Knife?*, that discussed the emotional responses of employees during periods of organizational downsizing.

At some moment during that lecture, I was hit by a lightning bolt, and I blurted out, "You're saying that this emotional response relates to the type of change employees experience during a layoff. Interestingly, I have been listening to employees dealing with technology change, organizational structure change, leadership change, reporting-status change, and process change since 1995, and they were all dealing with this 'blues' thing, too!"

Catching myself as I became aware of the abruptness of my interruption, I changed the tone of my voice. "Is it possible this type of depression is related to all types of change...that it is really not just a resistance to the change, but so much deeper than that?"

His gaze was fixed on me with a probing intensity, but after that prolonged moment of uncharacteristic silence, Dr. Harvey calmly responded, "Perhaps you have found a topic for your dissertation, Ms. Grady, and not only that, considering the intensity of your apparent convictions, perhaps you have found a lifelong research path as well."

PATRICK'S PROFESSIONAL INTEREST IN PEOPLE GETTING STUCK

My connection to the ideas behind *Stuck* came at a conference. I was struggling with two problems simultaneously – my clients were Stuck and I had too much data. I had been working with U.S. Federal Government clients for five years on change management programs around data and technology programs with little moderate success. While our direct clients loved our work, broad-based adoption of our solutions was always a challenge. I was struggling with a fundamental problem – leaders said they wanted more data-driven decision-making in federal organizations and most employees felt like they didn't understand why decisions were made.

To me, the solution was simple. If we used data to drive decisions, both sides would be happy! But every time we built a new data tool, the average employee rejected it. At the same time, my team had collected a mass of data from U.S. Federal Employees on their attitudes and engagement on the workplace. The data included over two million survey responses a year over five years. I believed there was a connection between these two problems, but I was not sure what.

I was at the Association of Change Management Professionals (ACMP) Global Conference in 2014 where my colleague Tim Creasey introduced me to this woman Victoria Grady. He told me she was a professor in the Washington, DC area and I had to go see her presentation. I said I would. As I mentioned previously, I try to keep my commitments to my friends. Victoria's presentation had two key components.

First, she explained the concept of attachment theory as why people had a negative biological reaction to change. *Check.* That solved one problem. I thought, "Of course people react negatively to new data tools. They know the data is better than their experience-based decision-making, that's not the point – it is new to them and that creates a sense of fear. It is a change."

Second, she described the framework behind the Change Diagnostic Index® (discussed more in Chapter 6), which is a survey-driven approach to understand how organizations are reacting to attachment. *Check.* Now I knew how we could use the Federal Employee data in a meaningful way for our overall agenda to support usage and adoption of new tools.

Victoria describes her reaction to Dr. Jerry Harvey as a lightning bolt striking. Well, lightning does strike the same place twice. It hit me too and the two of us began a collaboration that has lasted more than seven years of shared research, writing, presenting, teaching, and consulting. More importantly, this research and the concepts behind Stuck form the backbone of how I think about strategy, organizational change, digital transformation, and, yes, data analytics.

We have collaborated since that ACMP Conference on how to use the concepts and our joint research to create new insights for leaders and organizations. We have published several times, presented together, taught together, and collaborated on another (much more academic) book. But in this book our purpose is much different. We want to make our research practical. We want to make it so that anyone of any level in any organization can use our research to improve their work-life. We know how important and how hard it is to understand human behavior and the goal is to provide you with some insights to make it a little easier.

Being Stuck is a human experience. We have both been Stuck – obstinate and unwilling to change for no foreseeable reason – will be Stuck again, as will all of you. This is a human experience that we study to understand, but it is not going to go away. Hopefully you understand yourself, a co-worker, a leader, or your organization a little better at the end of this book. More importantly, we hope you are inspired to help make yourself, a co-worker, a leader, or your organization a little better based on something you read in this book.

Acknowledgments

Many people contributed to this work over the years. We are blessed to have so many people interested in this topic and contribute their time and stories. Many researchers and students have provided ideas, articles, and analysis over the years to support this work. Some of the most recent contributors were: Rachel Wittman, Ph.D. from Auburn University, Regan Jagatnarain, MBA from George Mason University, Tyece Wilkins, MBA Candidate from George Mason University, MaryJo Kolze, Ph.D. student at George Mason University, and the exceptional Colin Dosedel from Notre Dame.

Many colleagues have collaborated with us over the years to build on the ideas in this book. Again, a robust network of interested peers pushed on us to make the content and concepts we demonstrate here even stronger. First and foremost, James Grady, who has been a collaborator with Victoria for years and a collaborator with both of us on this book. His depth of research, understanding, and curiosity is inspiring. He brings so much passion and energy to his work. Tim Creasey, of Prosci, has always challenged us to take the extra step in logic and determine how to make the work more practical for the change management community. He is always willing to discuss any topic and test any idea. Ian Noakes provided critical contributions to the way that attachment styles evolve in the workplace and collaborated with us on our last book.

We have also had access to two wonderful institutions that have helped us build these ideas over the years. The first is George Mason University, where Victoria is an associate professor and Patrick holds an adjunct position. The students at George Mason University have been the testing ground of ideas for us both over the years and always provide excellent critical thinking and commentary on how to improve our concept. Additionally, the Association of Change Management Professionals (ACMP) has been an incubator of Stuck. It is the place where we met, we first presented together at an ACMP conference, we collected many of the stories in this book at ACMP events, we charted our first book at a conference, and we continue to learn and grow through the organization.

And then there are our personal sources of support.

For Victoria, this includes the Pivot Point Team and the incredible DHG Healthcare People and Change Team that includes Scott Spohn, Lydia Haas, and Christi Rich for our ongoing partnership that is so instrumental in the practical application of the research. My infinite love to David, Kendall, and Reagan for the 10+ years and countless hours of time I missed with you to finish the research that made this book possible. Thank you to my inspirational parents, specifically my Dad, James Grady, for his significant contributions to this work and my wonderful grandmother, Mimi, who always believed in me. Finally, to Jerry B. Harvey, your 2001 challenge "to learn to write…" and the subsequent loss of my beloved David J. Goetz in 2003 that were the basis of my inspiration for the research.

For Patrick, this includes my Simatree team that has worked with me and shown so much patience as we completed this book including my partner Wes Flores, Mellissa Perez, and Victoria Velasquez who all pick up the slack when I take on a new project. Thank you! Also, the incomparable Sarah Toigo who helps me find solutions through any design or intellectual challenge and contributed to the structure and design of this book. And to my family. Thank you for everything. My mother taught me what it means to never stop working and my late father's 42-year career as a leader showed me why people Stick to organizations. He built the kind of teams people want to join and I can only hope to live up to the model he set. Thank you to my sister, Erin, for being a sounding board for the many challenges of work and life we face today. To my daughters Lizzie, Rose, Bridget, and Ginger, thank you for sticking with me through this book. I know it hasn't always been easy, but your love, smiles, and snuggles instantly bring me back home after a busy day, week, or month. And to Courtney, my wife, thank you for everything you do for me and our family. You are the rock for us all. You make everything else possible.

Authors

Victoria M. Grady is the academic director of the MSM Graduate Program and associate professor of Management/Organizational Behavior in the School of Business at George Mason University. She also recently joined Dixon Hughes Goodman (DHG) based out of Charlotte, NC as the professor in residence for their People and Change Practice. Victoria's research portfolio focuses on the behavioral implications of organizations introducing and implementing organizational change – her unique emphasis is on the role of Attachment Behavior and Transitional Objects within the change process.

Victoria's consulting practice includes work with United States Federal Government agencies, private and public healthcare organizations in the United States and United Kingdom, utility organizations in Australia, k-12 and higher education institutions, nuclear power plants, and non-profit associations.

Recent research publications by Victoria can be found in *Harvard Business Review, Washington Business Journal, Bloomberg News*, GovExec. com, *the Journal of Change Management*, and *The Public Manager*. She is co-author of *The Pivot Point: Success in Organizational Change* (Morgan-James Publishing, 2013), co-author of *Family Capitalism: Best Practices in Ownership and Leadership* (Routledge, Gower Publishing, 2017), and *Attachment in the Workplace: Managing Beneath the Surface* (Routledge, Taylor and Francis Publishing, 2020). To learn more, please visit her website at www.pivotpnt.com, follow her on Twitter at @pivotpnt, or reach out via LinkedIN.

 **Patrick McCreesh**, Ph.D. is the managing partner of Simatree, a strategy, analytics, and technology consultancy. Patrick is a visionary in analytics and change management who passionately leads teams to build data-driven cultures. With 20 years of advisory experience, Patrick successfully leads teams through digital transformations and the development of analytics programs across the public sector and Fortune 500 clients.

Patrick serves as adjunct faculty at Georgetown University and George Mason University Business School. Previously, he published the book *Workplace Attachment: Managing Beneath the Surface* (Routledge, Taylor and Francis, 2019) and has had publications featured in *Bloomberg Government, the International Security Finance Monitor*, and *Public Manager*. Patrick is also a leader in the global change management community through the Association of Change Management Professionals (ACMP). He founded and served as the president of ACMP DC before serving on the ACMP Global Board of Directors.

Patrick graduated from The University of Virginia with a Bachelor of Arts in Foreign Affairs and History, received his Master of Public Policy from Harvard University, and completed his doctorate in Public Policy at George Mason University. He lives in Northern Virginia with his wife, Courtney, and four daughters – Lizzie, Rose, Bridget, and Ginger.

1

Why Do People Get Stuck?

"We're only as needy as our unmet needs."

John Bowlby

"Memory is the diary that we all carry about with us."

Oscar Wilde

"Oh Help! Oh Bother! I'm Stuck."

Winnie the Pooh

This book should have had a different opening. We were going to ask you to imagine a morning where your world had shifted. Where your routines were run amuck, your schedule disturbed, your very approach to work changed. Or maybe where you just woke up and couldn't find your phone. We would have asked you: How did you react? Of course, this is no longer some thought exercise. For most of us around the world, 2020 was a year when everything changed. So, how did you react?

What did you feel? Were you upset? Were you anxious? If you lost your job, how did you feel? If you worked from home, what did you miss? What did you long for? Was it a person you saw every day? Some item on your desk? A feeling of comfort in your position or role? Stability? Predictability? Childcare? Peace and quiet?

Through the ongoing global pandemic, we all lost something. Some were lucky to lose only the small comforts. Some lost much more. No matter the size of the loss, we all reacted with the same biological response. It is a biological response that has been with us since the early days of evolution. It resides in our brain. It explains how we form relationships with other people, with groups, and with organizations. This biological function explains how we perform, how we lead, how we motivate, and how we are

DOI: 10.4324/9781003157458-1

motivated. It explains how we respond to and engage with culture, and how we adapt to change. This biological mechanism explains why we sometimes embrace the shifting organizational landscape, but so often get Stuck.

Work is changing. Every day new companies, technologies, and ideas emerge that impact how and where we work. Technology companies and service providers were 42 of the Fortune 500 companies in 2020 and two of the three largest companies in the world (Amazon and Apple). More importantly, seven of the eight largest research and development budgets in the world belong to software, internet, and computing companies that in 2018 spent a staggering $107 billion on research and development.[1] The outlying company? Volkswagen, a car manufacturer that is trying to bring more technology into its brands. All this investment presents a range of opportunities for the future of our technology and work. Moreover, these stats were all pre-pandemic, before many organizational leadership teams were convinced that a technology-enabled and distributed workplace could be the future.

Despite this exciting evolution, people remain the heart of organizations. People are tricky. People don't seem to evolve as fast as our global environment. We get Stuck. Leaders, managers, and teammates struggle with resistance from their colleagues and get frustrated. Frustrated people dig in their heels and convince others. This impacts the performance of our organizations and now, instead of just a person being stuck, our whole organization is Stuck.

We set out to answer a seemingly simple question – *Why do people get Stuck?*

It turns out most people aren't actually Stuck; they are just going through a process. It is a deeply human process, even a biological process. It is rooted in our brain and the way our brain interacts with everything in the world, even work. It is how our brain controls our interactions with technology, our connection with peers, our perception of leaders, the way we view our organizations, and even our connection to the communities where we live. All of these factors impact how we perform as individuals at work and ultimately how organizations perform in the global marketplace.

We are not Stuck; we are working through a process of attachment and subsequent feelings of loss.

Attachment behavior is an instinctual response born out of our earliest days of life that impacts how we connect and interact with the world around us. Through this process, we are also introduced to loss. Those who learn to understand loss through attachment behavior and the attachments of others will succeed. The organizations, leaders, and managers who understand these concepts will evolve with the future. Those organizations that understand attachment can achieve business wins.

Loss is something we all know. Loss is when there is something you expected to be there that is unexpectedly gone. We have all felt it and understand what it does to us and to others. Just as the losses of the early days of the global pandemic required a massive shift in the way we work and operate, there are many other losses we have on a regular basis. Have you ever:

- Lost your keys?
- Misplaced your phone?
- Lost a family pet?
- Moved from one city to another?
- Moved locations at work from one floor to another?
- Watched your child go to their first day of kindergarten?
- Lost job responsibilities?
- Had a favorite leader re-assigned?

The feelings you had in these moments were probably not that different than the uncertainty you may have had in the early days of the pandemic. This sense of loss is attachment. It is a powerful biological instinct that impacts how we interact with people, organizations, and even communities. It is a normal part of human development and, here-to-now, it has been largely ignored in the workplace. But it shouldn't be ignored. It is the root of much behavior, and we simply must understand loss if we want to win at work.

BASEBALL, BOOKS, AND BLANKETS

As Billy Beane introduced the world of baseball to his unique and analytical style of managing a team, he also inspired a business and cultural revolution in the world of sports. Michael Lewis fully recounts the story in the book, *Moneyball*. The story follows the rise of the Oakland A's through the 2002 Major League Baseball season. The concept of analytics to determine the strategic direction of a sports team has since become a given. Basketball teams measure the release point of shots as a metric for offense and possible defense. Football's obsession with strength and speed has been enhanced with measures of angles and distance. While even tennis has gotten in the game by looking at common serve placements as a tool for defensive strategy.

The analytics of sports is everywhere, and the leaders in the space are seeking the non-obvious connections between data and results that will help them gain an edge. Sounds obvious today, but it was a battle for Billy.

Billy Beane was battling a 100-year-old (or more) way of thinking about how leaders build a team, how managers manage a game, and how pitchers and batters address an at bat. In short, Beane had to take on the culture of baseball. Players and talent scouts spent a lifetime developing their instincts for the game, and Beane undercut it all. Instead of leveraging hardened expertise, Beane and his team relied on the data to determine key decisions. They placed a bet that by using data, they could turn their mid-market team with one of the lowest total budgets into a competitor with the big guys.

Along the way, Billy had to change all the minds – the owners, the managers, the players, the media, and the fans. In the film version of *Moneyball*, this challenge comes to a head in a single moment when Beane is talking to an older scout, Grady. For years, scouts like Grady have been on the road looking for the next great talent. They have "an eye" and groom young, moldable, skilled men into baseball stars…sometimes. Sometimes it does not work out, and Billy was one that did not work out.

The conversation starts ominously when Grady says, "Billy, can we talk?"

Billy: You're unhappy

Grady: May I speak candidly?

Billy: Sure, go ahead

Grady: Major League Baseball and its fans are going to be more than happy to throw you and Google boy under the bus if you keep doing what you're doing here. You don't put a team together with a computer, Billy.

Billy: No?

Grady: No. Baseball isn't just numbers. It's not science. If it was than anyone could do what we're doing, but they can't because they don't know what we know. They don't have our experience and they don't have our intuition.

Billy: Okay...

Grady: Billy, you got a kid in there with an Economics degree from Yale. You got a scout here with 29 years of baseball experience. You are listening to the wrong one! Now, there are intangibles that only baseball people understand. You're discounting what scouts have done for 150 years, even yourself.

Billy: Adapt or die... [*with an emphatic hand clap.*]

Billy: You don't have a crystal ball. You can't look at a kid and predict his future any more than I can.

Grady: Major League Baseball thinks the way I think. You're not gonna win.

Grady goes on to provide some personal insults, to which Beane responds, "I'm not gonna fire you, Grady." Then the scout shoves him and Beane fires the scout.

Was the scout wrong? No. He had a strong, lifelong understanding of the game of baseball, and it made him a valuable asset to the A's organization. But Beane had a vision of what could be done in the future that conflicted with baseball's known and certain past. The scout represents a different type of attachment. For him, it is an attachment to culture, to what he knows, to the "way things have been done around here."

In 1999, when a student started college, they would go to the bookstore and dutifully find the books for the courses they were taking that semester down one of many rows of overflowing books. They would assess the total number of books for the class, the costs of these books, and they would decide whether to drop the class...kidding. They would pick up the many different books and ask a roommate to haul them back to the dorm to avoid the risk of injury in the first week of class.

Today, the incoming class of future graduates likely bought their books in their room and downloaded all the content to an e-reader with the only risk of injury being neck pain from laying awkwardly while looking for Thucydides. What happened?

We all know the story of the lost bookstore in the wake of Amazon and the shift to digital content, but let's look at the physical object of the e-reader. Prior to broad-based digital content, reading happened with a book. Snuggled up in bed or with a cup of coffee struggling to keep the right page while balancing the other aspects of life. And while the digital revolution is partly to account for today's success in digital books, something else happened. The e-reader.

Today, there are two camps in the world of voracious readers. The loyalist books camp and the new age e-reader camp. The loyalists are dealing with an attachment to both an object (the book) and a preferable experience (the act of holding the book). The new age readers have moved past this attachment into the era of the e-reader. But were they destined to be digital readers? Probably not. Reading on a computer screen is a very different experience from reading a physical book. One must sit up in bed with the computer on your lap or worse, sit at a desk.

The e-reader is not simply a digital format, it is the recreation of the written word consumption that book readers love … in a digital format. In fact, even the language of the e-reader implies that the device is meant to be something other than a book or computer. It is called "Paperwhite," "Nook," or "Boox." It can be snuggled with, and it can sit next to your coffee while you contemplate whether your characters really should do what they just did.

For both camps in this new religious war, the physical object has become the attachment. The words are the same, the story is the same, and even the experience is the same. But each prefers their way of reading. For the books camp, it is a little attachment to the culture of books in addition to the object. For the e-reader crowd, they have found what we call a "transitional object." This is a new physical object that takes the place of a former attachment and helps ease the sense of loss that comes with a new way of doing things.

Billy and Grady's exchange may sound familiar. It happens at work on a regular basis. There is tension between new and old ways of doing work. Digital vs. Paper. Data vs. Intuition. Automation vs. Manual. Maybe you are an e-reader or a book loyalist. You may have these conversations on a regular basis with your parents, your children, or your friends. But it may also remind you of something more basic.

Have you ever watched a child hold a cherished toy or blanket tight? Have you ever seen a child in panic trying to find their favorite stuffed animal right before bed? It's not too different from watching an adult who has lost (or temporarily misplaced) their phone. The panic and sense of anxiety is real. There is a sense of loss.

No one was better at watching, understanding, and mirroring children than Charles Schulz, the creator of Charlie Brown and *Peanuts*. And he also understood attachment. That's right. The cartoonist. His *Peanuts* showed the life and development of children in simple drawings with complex themes. Charlie Brown and his dog Snoopy explore the wider world of suburbia with a cast of friends who represent the myriad of possible personalities born from just a few simple pen strokes. But each character is much more complex and effectively represents adult behavior.

One character with such complexity is Linus Van Pelt. He references philosophers and poets, worships the coming of the Great Pumpkin, and serves as the voice of reason to remind the children of the true meaning of Christmas. And Linus has one companion through all his journeys – his baby blue blanket.

The blanket goes everywhere and serves as a prop for Linus in many facets of life. He uses it as a headdress, a slingshot, a hammock, a kite, a sports coat, and a scarf. Linus finds any occasion to ensure the blanket's close contact and often doubles the comfort with a thumb in his mouth. The blanket first appeared on June 1, 1954, in a four-panel comic strip. Charlie Brown asks Linus's sister Lucy, "Why does Linus hold his blanket like that?" In the second panel, she responds, "I'm not sure … I think maybe it gives him a feeling of security." In the third panel Charlie Brown walks away from Lucy. In the final panel, we see him holding his own blanket as he exclaims, "It doesn't work … I feel like an idiot!"

Linus and his blanket popularized the term "security blanket," and it seems Schulz intended to make the connection to attachment. Schulz regularly played bridge with a neighbor, Fritz Van Pelt (the same last name used for Linus). During their repeated sessions, Schulz would hide the favorite stuffed animal of Van Pelt's daughter. The elder Van Pelt once told Schulz that he should stop doing it. He explained that the stuffed animal is an important bridge between the parent and the rest of the world. Van Pelt had read some studies in psychology and explained the work of D. W. Winnicott, who studied security in children. Schulz took it to heart and created Linus's "security blanket."[2]

As critic and novelist Sarah Boxer notes, "Linus knew that he could take his blows philosophically … as long as he had his security blanket nearby."[3] As the comic evolves, so does Linus's devotion to the blanket. It becomes more intense. He chooses the blanket over everything – toys, love interests, even his favorite teacher. It is not a "nice to have;" it is a necessity. In a later strip he threatens the lovable Snoopy for even eyeing the blanket. Linus warns, "Make one move toward this blanket, you stupid beagle, and I'll destroy all hopes you have for the future!"

Again, we see a common theme. In a world of only children (the adults never appear in the cartoon), one child demonstrates the challenges of loss. This is not to say attachment is a childish feeling. It is not. Attachment is a human behavior that is illustrated through the child of Linus. What Linus holds in his blanket is a transitional object, which is a powerful tool for supporting individuals through the process of loss and change. Adults today have many physical objects that help them through periods of loss in the workplace. Whether it is following the loss of a leader, a trusted software, or a job responsibility, the idea of transitional objects is to serve as the security blanket for the team member who is struggling with the change.

These three stories about baseball, books, and blankets present characters who have an attachment to something in their lives – a person, a culture, or an object – that they do not want to let go. Attachments are not bad, they just are. These attachments provide support (many times unconsciously) in the face of change.

The scout's attachment for the Oakland A's has positive qualities. Attachment to culture is valuable for sustaining a well-established and proven way of doing things. Many companies would love to have this level of commitment from their workforce, but it is an attachment that yields tension when there is a new vision or approach to the future that is introduced. Again, this attachment is not bad, it just must be understood.

In the war for the written word, both camps have attachments to objects. Both are right (and potentially wrong) to have these attachments. For the e-readers of the world, that attachment provides a sense that things have not changed that much, they just have greater access to information, faster. For book lovers, things haven't changed that much, as they still have their books (for most titles).

Like the book lovers and e-readers, Linus has found his object that helps him through the tough times. His security blanket helps him connect with the world around him while holding some confidence in tiny hand.

As it is with these three examples, so it is with the workers in our global organizations. We all have attachments. They are not good or bad. They just are. But, when you are trying to make a change, it is likely these attachments may be the visible signs of the deeper process of attachment. Visuals like a commitment to baseball, blankets, or books might be a sign that someone is Stuck.

How to Work with Stuck

The purpose of our work is to answer the question: *Why do people get Stuck?*

The purpose of this book is to explain how our work and the research we have conducted can help you more effectively manage yourself, your teams, and your organization.

As such, this book is full of academic research that is distilled into practical lessons. We are sharing with you more than 20 years of research, data gathering, and consulting engagements through stories that we hope will make the concepts more relatable and workable in your organization. Victoria has developed three different survey-based assessments that she has administered to over 20,000 respondents across 150 organizations over the last 20 years. Patrick has advised C-suite executives in the private sector and the public sector on strategy, change management, and the use of analytics. Together, we have applied our methodology to a massive dataset of public sector personnel and used our research in the instruction of hundreds of academic and private sector students. We use the feedback from all of these engagements to improve and enhance our research. This book includes lessons and original stories from the application of attachment concepts in more than 150 organizations across all sectors around the globe.

The best way to think of this book is as a modern playbook for managing an organization by starting with the brain. We hope it provides a more detailed approach to concepts you may already know intuitively or at a base level, and gives you the rationale, research, or data to support what you have felt. We want this book to help you where you are and we know people engage differently. As such, this book includes many different ways to engage with the concepts: Some sections based in theory, some based on stories, and some based on data. Read what works for you.

Like a playbook, we are also giving you ways to practice and apply what you have learned throughout the book. We want this to be an experience for you through which you can grow in your understanding of the concepts and also apply them directly to your life. Each chapter ends with a few Practical Exercises that will help you Reflect, Observe, Collect, Apply, or Analyze some component of the chapter. Most of these can be done alone but, in some cases, we provide options for you to try the activities in a group.

So, *why do people get Stuck?*

It is due to a process called attachment that starts in the Limbic System of our brain, this is our Intuitive Brain. *Attachment is the human need to lean on tangible and/or intangible objects for support.* We will start the next chapter by explaining how the journey of the brain led us to attachment:

- The Brain's Journey Is Our Journey (Chapter 2)
- Why Do I Get Stuck? (Chapter 3)
- How Do I Get Stuck? (Chapter 4)
- What Do I Get Stuck To? (Chapter 5)
- How Does Culture Get Stuck? (Chapter 6)
- Is My Organization Stuck? (Chapter 7)
- Leading a Stuck Organization (Chapter 8)
- Unsticking the Future (Chapter 9)

In Chapter 2, we will explain how the brain evolved from its primitive beginnings and focus on survival to become a complex calculator of social algorithms. In this chapter, you will learn how the Intuitive Brain formed and how this part of the brain serves our attachment process today. This is the part of the brain where we get Stuck.

In the next few chapters, we will focus on how attachment relates to you, as an individual. We will describe the attachment process in Chapter 3 and how it forms from our earliest day as an infant and evolves through our life. We will see how attachment stays with us as we grow into adults and continues with us to the workplace. We will explore how attachment and loss are connected, and which attachment symptoms reveal themselves as we experience loss. We will also learn that attachments form and shift as we grow, meaning that attachments can be shaped. From this, we will learn the critical role that experience plays in attachment, leading to different attachment styles and favoritism for different attachment objects (our next two chapters).

In Chapter 4, we will learn that not all people have the same type of attachment style. This means we Stick differently. We will learn some of

the advantages and disadvantages of different attachment styles to understand how we might work with different styles in the workplace. We will
share what we have seen from an assessment called the Attachment Styles
Index ©. There is even an opportunity to assess yourself and see what
this might tell you about how you behave in the workplace based on your
attachment style.

In Chapter 5, we will move on to the objects that support us through
the attachment process. Here we will learn the different types of objects –
people, places, things, ideas – that we lean on for support in organizations.
We will also discuss the important role of objects in helping people transition from a Current State to a Future State. These transitional objects are a
special type of object in the attachment space; they are tools in the arsenal
of change leaders. Again, we will provide you the opportunity to assess
yourself and try to discuss some of your preferences for attachment objects.

Over the following three chapters, we will move from the individual to
the organization. Chapter 6 takes on the light topic of culture. Peter Drucker
wrote that "Culture eats strategy for breakfast," but he also said "Company
cultures are like country cultures. Never try to change one. Try, instead, to
work with what you've got." We try to take a more hopeful view and explain
why an attachment-based understanding of culture helps demystify what
culture is within an organization and therefore makes it more possible to
shape organizational culture. In this chapter, we will explore some of the
key elements of culture that support a co-creation approach to culture. In
this way, leaders can help create a culture that Sticks without creating a culture that makes people feel Stuck.

Chapter 7 is about what happens when organizations get Stuck. This
chapter highlights data from the Change Diagnostic Index©, a survey
that has been taken by more than 18,000 people across 125 organizations.
We will see how leadership emerges as the top challenge for managing
attachment at the organizational level. We will discuss how attachment
challenges emerge at all levels of leadership and some of the ways these
can be mitigated. In Chapter 7, we give you the opportunity to assess your
organization and determine what attachment challenges you may be likely
to face within your organization.

In Chapter 8, we will focus on the tools that leaders need to work *with*
attachment behavior to support people and create healthy attachments in
organizations. We will outline five critical tools to implement organizational change. We will discuss how common tools like communication,

training, and performance management can be enhanced through a better understanding of attachment. Additionally, we will re-frame the critical role of leadership and transitional objects in the context of major organizational change programs.

Last, in Chapter 9, we will try to predict the future, or at least learn from the recent past. We will look at some of the trends in organizations to understand how an attachment lens helps leaders and employees respond differently to particular situations. Whether it is the recent pandemic, the challenge to diversify our organizations, the need to become more data-driven, or the desire to build resiliency; our organizations need to evolve to become nimbler. For this to happen, people need to become more aware of their own attachments and what keeps them Stuck.

Many people feel Stuck. Stuck in their jobs, Stuck in different parts of work, Stuck in their ability to move programs and projects along. Stuck in their ability to drive change. Do you feel Stuck?

What if there was one little biological function that determines how well you will perform at work, how well you will interact with others in the workplace, how well you lead, how well you follow, how well you assimilate to the culture of an organization, and most importantly … how well you adapt to a change? What if one biological function could explain all that? Would you want to understand it? Or would you be content to stay where you are? Will you stay … Stuck?

PRACTICAL EXERCISES

REFLECT: GETTING STUCK

The process of getting Stuck to relationships and organizations happens over time. This first reflection is a warm-up exercise to get you in the habit of thinking about your past and how it impacts where you are today. There are two possible ways to think about this. You can choose to think about a relationship, or you can think about your work organization. Pick one (or do both, we won't know). Now, answer the questions below based on which one you chose:

Relationship

Do you remember your first interaction with the person?

Do you remember your first sight, sound, smell with the person?

What is the emotion you recall in this relationship with the person?

What is the first shared experience you recall with the person (something you did together)?

How long have you had this relationship?

How would you describe your relationship with the person today?

How would you describe your emotions about this person today?

If someone saw this relationship from the outside, how would they describe it?

Organization

Do you remember your first interaction with the organization (met at a conference, saw an ad, a recruiting event, an interview event, outreach)?

Do you remember the first visual you saw from the organization or person you met from the organization?

What is the emotion you recall in your initial interactions with this first person or group of people?

How would you describe this person or group of people?

How long have you been with the organization?

Would you describe yourself as similar to the person or group of people you first met from the organization?

How would you describe your emotions about the organization today?

How would an outsider describe the organization?

How would an outsider describe your relationship with the organization?

 REFLECT: SOMETHING CHANGED, PART 1

Do you remember a time that something significant changed at your work? It might be at your current organization or at a former organization.

- What was the change that happened?
- How big was the change? How many people did it impact in the organization?
- How did it personally impact you?
- How did you feel about the change?
- Were you quick to adapt to the change or were you slow to change?
  - If you were quick, do you know why?
  - If you were slow, do you know why?
- What about other people in the organization; were they quick to adapt to the change or were they slow?
  - If they were quick, do you know why?
  - If they were slow, do you know why?

Consider writing down some thoughts about this now.

Seriously. We are going to come back to this topic in future chapters, so it would be good to be able to reference your initial reactions.

NOTES

1 "Top 1000 Companies that Spend the Most on Research & Development (Charts and Analysis)." Idea to value.com. Accessed electronically on July 3, 2021, at: www. ideatovalue.com/inno/nickskillicorn/2019/08/top-1000-companies-that-spend-the-most-on-research-development-charts-and-analysis/.

2 Kramer, P. (2019). "Nonsense!" *The Peanuts Papers*. Ed. A. Blauner. New York: Library of America.

3 Boxer, S. (2019). "The Exemplary Narcissism of Snoopy." *The Peanuts Papers*. Ed. A. Blauner. New York: Library of America.

2

The Brain's Journey Is Our Journey

"In all social species that have been observed … it is clear that the group possesses a protective function for the individuals that comprise it …. It is thus reasonable to believe that there is some basic behavioral system that has evolved in social species that leads individuals to seek and maintain proximity to [a group of] conspecifics."

Mary Ainsworth[1]

"Today, humanity is like a waking dreamer, caught between the fantasies of sleep and the chaos of the real, we have created a Stars Wars civilization, with Stone Age emotions, medieval institutions, and godlike technology"

E. O. Wilson[2]

Madalyn is the senior vice president for sales and strategy for the Midwest region of a nationwide insurance carrier. She has a great track record of collaborating with partners to drive sales and a 10-year history of hitting the annual target of five to seven percent growth expected by her leadership team. Madalyn's approach stems from her long-term relationships with channel partners that help her leverage relationships with larger organizations to drive sales, resulting in the highest sales in her division. She builds relationships over nine to 12 months to strike a deal with a channel partner that will increase sales by one percent in the next year.

As 2019 started, Madalyn was coming off the best year of her career. She just hit 10 percent growth and she had channel partners lined up to yield another eight percent, exactly on track with corporate expectations. At the end of Q1, at the leadership team meeting, the national sales president noted that sales were lagging across the country and that the team may need to think about strategies to improve sales by the end of the year.

DOI: 10.4324/9781003157458-2

Madalyn wasn't seeing the same trends; she was still on target and she saw nothing to slow her down. All she had to do was stay the course.

Madalyn came to the Q2 leadership meeting proud of her success. She was ahead of plan because one of the channel partners she expected to join in Q3 unexpectedly started early. But she heard a different tone at the meeting. Again, the national sales president expressed concern, but this time he also adjusted targets for the regions that were doing well. Instead of eight percent growth, Madalyn would need to hit the 10 percent growth she found in 2018. Additionally, Madalyn's success with channel partners was highlighted and the national sales president asked Madalyn if she could use any of her channel relationships to drive sales in other regions.

By the Q3 meeting, the situation was dire. Madalyn's peers were deeply behind plan. Every other region was missing their targets. Madalyn was still hitting her eight percent target for growth but saw no way to hit a 10 percent target. While she tried to have her channel partners support sales in other regions, it was mostly met with resistance. It turns out that her channel partners were aligned by region too and they had little incentive to support the growth of other regions.

In the middle of the Q4, the national sales president called a meeting. The company was being sold to a competitor. The low production across the board was a sign that the company could no longer compete. Most of the sales team would be considered duplicative, but the acquiring company had minimal presence in the Midwest. The national sales president told Madalyn the acquirer was quite excited to meet Madalyn to see how she could help them build their presence.

Madalyn's story is common, but it is also the story of our brain. The human brain has been slowly moving down an evolutionary path for millennia. Our brain set a singular target – survival – and drove toward that target from the beginning of time. The brain evolved to meet the demands of other functions in society, but only so far as it serves this central goal of survival.

We all know the story of the tortoise and the hare. The tortoise slowly plods along in the race while the hare speeds ahead only to take a rest and he wakes up to find the tortoise crossing the finish line in the end. That is how organizations behave with the brains of their employees. Organizations speed along expecting to beat the brains of employees to the finish line, but the brain slowly plods along and wins every time. What do we mean by win? Organizations can't move faster than the brain. In fact, an organization that needs people to progress can't move forward faster than that slowest critical brain.

The brain's singular purpose remains to help one individual navigate the world for survival. We have oversimplified the brain in our organizations to talk about rational behavior and emotional behavior. In reality, the brain is a complex web of filters and blurred processes, where the rational brain is filtered by perception and intuition and the emotional brain is blurred by history and nurturing. Within this complex web exists an Intuitive Brain that is the source of our memory, emotions, and learning – and here is where we get Stuck.

In this chapter we will explore:

- What does evolution teach us about the brain and how it's functions developed?
- How do rational and emotional functions work in the brain?
- What does modern research tell us about the brain?
- How does the brain get Stuck?
- How can I begin to assess my own brain and my rational/emotional challenges?

OUR EVOLUTION LED TO THE BRAIN WE HAVE

Our organizations attempt to evolve at a blistering pace, but we are stuck with a brain that has evolved at a glacial pace. When you think of human evolution, you undoubtedly get the visual of the monkey evolving to the modern man. The first steps in that path were the early primates who began their move from crawl to walk about 22 million years ago. Many of the critical traits that support human development happened over the next 20 million years, as these ancestors evolved into the early Homo species that we think of today.

These early humans used their brain power for one thing – survival! Around two million years ago, three Homo species emerged with notice-able larger brains. As our brains enlarged the brain required more energy. The energy could not be attained by a plant-based diet, which led to the need for more protein. These species became dependent on animals for both the protein to drive increased brain energy and the amino acids to support brain development. Of course, an individual could not simply gather enough food for oneself for a long period of time, so the notion of cooperation developed.

Evolutionarily speaking, humans did not have physical advantages. We had minimal biological defensive characteristics and were not able to overpower most of the prey we sought. However, we did have cleverness and, more importantly, the means to work with others that allowed us to collaborate and cooperate toward a shared purpose. That shared purpose was initially the hunt and survival, but evolved overtime into more robust endeavors.[3]

The brain required more energy to fuel its development into a more complex biological instrument. The human brain evolved with three distinct components or layers that track the evolutionary path – *the reptilian brain, the mammalian brain, and the cortical brain.* The reptilian brain is often described as the habit-forming part of the brain that focuses on our most basic Maslowian needs, like thirst, hunger, sexuality, and shelter. The physical structure here is the basal ganglia. As we evolved, we developed the mammalian brain, which brings in the functions of memory and learning. This sits directly between the other two parts of the brain. As we will see in a moment, there is more at play here, but for now this simple definition will do.

In the third area of the brain, we find the bulk of the brain's mass, the part that needed to be fed with all that protein, called the cortical brain. The cerebral cortex represents more than 40 percent of the mass of the brain and is where the central nervous system comes to a head (pun intended). It is within the mass of nerves that attention, perception, awareness, thought, language, and indeed consciousness itself all come life. It was in this third area of the brain where human society as we think of it, and the workplace as we know it, started to emerge. As the larger cortical brain developed, our meat-eating ancestors had both the biological need to collaborate *and* the biological capacity to collaborate. Their growing cortical capacity allowed for the development of social interactions, more complex hunting strategies, and communication skills.

While collaboration began for the hunt, it quickly spread into a host of other activities to support social development. Some individuals began to focus on hunting, while others would focus on protecting the children. Instead of chasing the animals, these early species would begin to build more permanent campsites. Over time, some members of the group would hunt, and some would farm. In modern shorthand, we start to see division of labor and specialization of work that further supported the advancement of the society.

In the development of these distinct roles, many of these early humans undoubtedly started to develop routines. The reptilian brain focuses on base survival, but the mammalian brain focuses on memory and learning. It is in this space of the brain where our earliest ancestors started to build basic routines and habits. As Shawn Achor notes, "Humans... are biologically prone to habit, and it is because we are 'mere bundles of habits' that we are able to automatically perform many of our daily tasks ..."[4] These early ancestors became defined by their roles and what they did in their society.

Additionally, the more advanced brain led to more advanced social interactions. With each new cortical connection, new human connections were also formed, and this ability became a critical part of success in emerging societies. Connections to other people became central to the survival of each person and to the people around them. As John Bowlby notes, "Humans are by instinct a group animal. To survive, [earliest mankind was] ... equipped with [attachment] systems that provide effective protection, and this group living arrangement provides that function."[5]

All of these functions were supported by a slowly advancing brain that evolved over nearly 22 million years from a primitive state focused on thirst and hunger to one that could specialize and strategize, communicate and collaborate. But this took 22 million years of evolution and many potential candidates for the evolutionary frontrunner failed along the journey. Therefore, we cannot breeze through these few paragraphs and expect the journey to extend indefinitely in our lifetime. No, we need to acknowledge the impressive progress of the brain, but ultimately, we need to take the brain as it is today.

WE COME TO WORK WITH THE BRAIN WE HAVE

The brain developed through evolution in three parts – *reptilian, mammalian, and cortical* – but is often studied via 14 anatomical features or functions. These include functions like smell, hearing, speech formation, vision, voluntary movement, and so on. In the workplace, we tend to ignore both constructs to talk about the brain with two main components – the rational brain and the emotional brain. In colloquial terms, we tend to speak of the rational side as working through life with logic, order, and reason. The other version is the emotional side where we react out of feeling and sentiment.

This dichotomy is flawed. There truly are three parts of the brain. In the 1950s the American neurologist Paul MacLean coined the term Triune Brain that closely mirrors the evolutionary path. He describes the reptilian (instinctive) brain, the mammalian (emotional) brain, and the cortical (human/rational) brain. However, over time, we have learned much more about the mammalian brain and to label it as the emotional brain does the systems of our brain a disservice.[6]

It is truly an *Intuitive Brain*, as we will show, that brings together much more power and challenge to the workplace. *Intuition* resides in the Limbic System of the brain where the learning processes and memory are co-located with emotion. This makes sense because intuitive processes are developed through learned behavior. The Limbic System resides between the cortical and reptilian brains working between the two to store information into implicit memory from the intensive processing of rationality and moving associations closer to the survival instincts of our reptilian brains. It is this Intuitive Brain that drives the positive and negative nature of our Stickiness.

A critical part of the Limbic System is the hippocampus. The hippocampus supports an important type of neuroplasticity, which is when our brains neural networks change and adjust. In particular, we experience a type of neuroplasticity called long-term potentiation (LTP). LTP occurs when we convert short-term memories into long-term memories. For many who study habit formation, the hippocampus is the key to turning a desire to take on a new behavior into the intuitive process of doing the new behavior.

As we will see, the three-part brain is not a set of unique components of a computer sending data from one system to another. Instead, it is a complex set of systems working together, but ultimately blurred by learned memory and emotion. As these systems interact, the Intuitive Brain is simultaneously relying on memory, emotions, and associations while trying to learn in the current space. What sits between all of this emotion and rationality is attachment that supports our learning and growth, but also becomes the key to understanding why people get Stuck.

The Rational Brain

We tend to think of our rational brain as the thinking part of the brain where we make decisions based on data and logic. The *reasoning* part of the brain is where we make tradeoffs and decisions with logic and reason. The decision-making elements of the cortical network reside in the pre-frontal cortex. These are the elements of the brain that focus on judgment, personality, and voluntary movement. Reasoning is inherently a slow process whereby our brain must process information and must bring this information together through a series of processes to compare this information against each other into order to decide.

Basic economics provides us a pure version of how the rational brain works. It is a tradeoff for a rational actor. Economics describes the rational actor as one with a set of preferences that will act on these preferences to make the necessary tradeoffs and get what is most advantageous for that actor.

A simple example happens at the grocery store. Imagine yourself in the cereal aisle making a decision about cereal for yourself. You list your objectives for your purchase. Of course, you need a certain amount of energy for that big brain you are carrying around, you may want to minimize sugar to watch your waistline or maximize it to hide the taste of things that are good for you, and you might be thinking about cost. The rational actor would take each box and calculate the best cereal to meet the objectives you laid out on some sort of metric like calories per penny.

Of course, we don't see people sitting in the cereal aisle with calculators. They grab a box and go. That's because the reasoning side of the brain uses filters to make the processes move much faster. In 1957, the economist Herb Simon introduced the concept of bounded rationality. Simon argues that we choose from a set of limited options based on limited information with limited preferences. Simon also notes that the limited human mental capacity requires us to limit our choices. Sticking with our cereal example, one of the important variables in the reasoning process is **time**. Our brain lacks the ability to calculate the cost per calorie of each cereal in the time it would take to make the decision about which cereal to purchase. Therefore, our reasoning has some bounds to it and we use other filters to make our decision. Maybe it is relying on known brands, trusted flavors, or simply colorful boxes.

The Intuitive Brain's Role in Reasoning

This is where the Intuitive Brain steps into the role of the rational brain. Unlike the reasoning part of the brain, the intuitive part of the brain is fast. It is does not requiring the processing of information; instead, it simply reacts in a seamlessly automatic fashion to the surroundings. The most common example we use of intuitive processes tends to be "riding a bike." Despite the fact this requires our brain to coordinate many tasks and functions simultaneously it is so commonly referred to as the example of the intuitive skill coming back to us. Maybe it's not as simple as riding a bike.

Daniel Kahneman and Amos Tversky deeply explored intuition through their lifetime of Nobel-prize winning work on intuition and the psychological factors that contribute to our behavior in the economy. Their work demonstrates how the mind impacts our choices and leads us to make

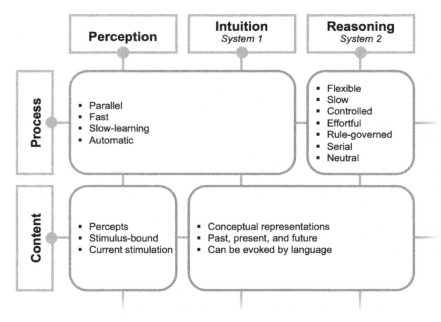

FIGURE 2.1
Three Cognitive Systems.[8]

judgments. They argue that our brain develops ways of navigating the world around us by limiting, shaping, and scoping information to make the vast amounts of it manageable and still be able to make reasonable decisions (Figure 2.1). Those tasks or activities that we learn to do without even thinking become intuitive and no longer require the rational reasoning.[7]

In the workplace, these intuitive activities happen on a regular basis. Depending on where our work resides in the economic spectrum, these intuitive activities may be the core of your work. A manufacturing job or an administrative processing role may need you to complete the same activity repeatedly everyday as an intuitive task. Many in the knowledge economy may have a job description that seemingly has no intuitive activities. However, large organizations often require a set of administrative functions that become intuitive to the members of that organization, similar to our earliest ancestors and their understanding of roles in the hunting and gathering process. These learned functions become intuitive tasks even in what may seem to be a critical-thinking role.

Another critical filter in the reasoning process are mental models. Mental models serve as an internal algorithm or schema for how to handle the world around us. Mental models are an example of the intuitive cognitive process that help filter and sort information. These not only support decision-making, like our trivial cereal example, but also everyday navigation of the world for survival. Frost on the lawn means it is cold, get a jacket. There is a puddle in the road that could be deep, slow down. Mental models are rarely built on single attributes, but rather a set of attributes combined to create our understanding of a situation – like a complex mathematical algorithm. Many of the different attributes we learn to identify fall into binary pairs like light–dark, safe–unsafe, or weak–strong. But it is not the single pairs that make the mental models. It is the combinations of pairs that really demonstrate the strength of the human brain.

For example, when we are watching a horror movie and we suddenly get the sense that something terrible is going to happen. That sense does not come from rationally examining the plot of the film, it is because we have been trained to understand that the combination of a dark alley with eerie music, a blowing wind, and a protagonist walking alone may lead to danger. It is the interaction of signals that create the mental model.

The same is true within organizations where we use mental models to interact with customers and co-workers, and make decisions. Unlike the intuitive tasks that are the formal roles of the job, the mental models of the workplace are how to navigate the role or organization. For example, a person may be taught the functional steps to be a salesclerk, but that will not suffice for how to work with customers. The employee will also need to learn how to "read" people in the context of the store environment. Is the customer happy with the service of the store or disappointed? Is the customer struggling to understand the cost? Is the customer struggling to understand the employee? Mental models emerge for these situations as the brain starts to understand how to work within the situation.

Mental models extend to interactions with co-workers. We use mental models to learn how to identify extroverts and introverts, to identify skillsets and strengths in other people, and to understand how we will build our own response to others. Mental models are critical functions that help us navigate an organization. Simply think of titles. When a soldier hears the rank of commanding officer in the military, or an employee sees a title like chief technology officer; they intuitively know the importance of the person.

There is an important distinction to make here, especially when talking about people. Mental models are NOT stereotyping but may be a precursor to stereotypes from a biological perspective. We are NOT talking about how to proliferate negative or systematic beliefs about groups of individuals. Mental models are the short cuts our brains will use to manage the vast amounts of information available to us in the world. Stereotyping is a possible negative downside of mental models that individuals and leaders must avoid. Our brains our wired to find short cuts and as we interact with employees in organizations, we have a responsibility to avoid proliferating broad concepts that others can potentially catalogue as a mental model to discriminate against others.

Mental models also impact the decision-making processes in organizations. Just as we develop models for people, we develop analogues for situations. These analogues are helpful to speed decision-making. It is as if the brain knows it has seen this situation before and it is applying the same principles it applied that last time to this decision. For example, when deciding where to place a new location, the vice president of operations for a growing retail workout apparel chain will likely look at the customers in recent locations and try to find locations with similar demographics, square footage, and a similar environment. What if there is a factor that is not revealed by this methodology? What if growth in the past three stores was enabled by social media influencers in the same location? How would that data get introduced into the decision-making framework?

There are many common mental models we employ in our organizations. We tend to combine them with processes to help us implement the model. For example, in budgeting we often claim we are building a return-on-investment budget, but we really take last year's budget and add to it through a mental model of incrementalism. We often bring models around tradeoffs. We tend to discount certain factors based on what we believe about the future, which can lead to either optimistically developing financial outlooks for the future or developing more pessimistic views. No matter how these are deployed, the mental models become almost like a filter over our decision-making process that can shape the information we review, but also can limit our information review.

The Emotional Brain

The emotional brain is defined as the reactive state whereby emotions govern the behavior of individuals. The reality of emotion is much more complicated than that. The emotional brain is a part of the brain responsible for interpreting signals from the vast environment around the body using all the available sensors (eyes, ears, mouth, nose, skin) and associating these sensations with past experiences and anatomical functions to understand what type of response the body should provide to the situation.

As James Grady outlines, the simple act of reading someone's facial expression to understand our own response is a complicated process. The information of the other person's facial expression must move through a "lattice of facial recognition networks related to recognition of the meaning of various expressions" in our reptilian brain to determine whether the other person is a threat. This basic function supports survival before a response is considered. Then a secondary function can be activated in the cortex to determine (once safety is assured) the appropriate response. These emotional signals get categorized by the brain into a set of emotional processes. This is the point when all of the understanding of expressions and the environment pivots to response.[9]

Estonian neuroscientist Jaak Panskeep devoted his life's work to studying the brain's reaction to the environment to understand emotions. His research started by looking at the emotional brains of animals via MRI

TABLE 2.1

Executive Emotional Systems (Traditionally in All Caps)

System	Affective Description	Negatives	Extreme
SEEKING	Enthusiasm and motivation	Frustration	Obsessive Compulsive Addiction
RAGE	Anger and irritability	Contempt	Aggression
FEAR	Worry and concern	Anxious	Phobias Psychic trauma PTSD
LUST	Erotic feeling	Jealousy	Fetishes
CARE	Tender and loving	Romantic attachment	Dependency disorders
PANIC	Lonely and sad	Guilt and shame	Depression
PLAY	Joyous	Overactive	ADHD

scans and he was able to evolve this research into solutions for the human brains that might be struggling with some sort of addiction or loss. Through his years of research, he isolated our emotional processes into seven primal emotional systems (Table 2.1). These are the core emotions that sit at the root of our responses and Panskeep studied these to understand how brains behaved when each of these emotions were activated. All these emotions have necessary roles in our lives. They also have negative sides that can create challenges in organizations or workplaces and extremes that can create personal challenges for individuals.[10]

The Intuitive Brain's Role in Emotions

Unfortunately for us, the emotional systems do not seem to be treated equally by our brains. There is a hierarchy that exists and some of it is intuitive. Our more basic primitive emotional responses of FEAR, RAGE, and LUST reside in the reptilian brain where the brain does not temper reactions, but just reacts. The other four emotional systems of SEEKING, CARE, PANIC, and PLAY, that all have a more social element, reside in the Limbic System. These are tempered and influenced by our other associations and memories.

Note that none of these emotion systems reside in the cortical brain. Our rational brain with its logic and reason cannot control emotions. It does control response, so the brain can learn to temper these emotions, but all the strength and power of the meat-fed cortical brain can only dampen the impact of our core emotional systems. These systems are reactions that are formed biologically based on the brain. Our three primitive emotional systems of FEAR, RAGE, and LUST existing in the reptilian brain are more hardwired, based on nature. However, the other four system are clearly connected to nurture.

Our social emotional systems exist in the Limbic System. This is critically important because the Limbic System is the place where memory, emotions, and learning come together in the brain. Our social emotional systems of SEEKING, CARE, PANIC, and PLAY are necessarily informed by the events of our lives and the associations we bring from these events. From an early age, these four systems are engaged by the people around us – parents, family members, and caretakers. The way in which these individuals engage our social emotional systems will determine how we develop them.

Effective early parenting and caretaking will lead to SEEKING systems that are enthusiastic, CARE systems that are tender and loving, PANIC systems that are calm, and PLAY systems that are joyful and measured. On the outside, this will look like a parent who is supporting a child with effective skills and social development. Within the child's Limbic System, the brain will be learning what are good versions of each of these systems, storing that information in the memory, and associating certain sights, sounds, and anatomical response to those emotions. These will be stored for life.

We should repeat … these will be stored for life.

HOW THE INTUITIVE BRAIN GETS STUCK

The Intuitive Brain (our Limbic System) supports both our reasoning and emotional functions. It is a force on its own. It is also the source of our attachments. Attachments are the tangible and intangible objects we lean on for support as we navigate the world. Attachments form as a learned experience that is a combination of memory and emotion. In this way, they are incredibly powerful because they work in the Limbic System where all the social emotional functions reside. Therefore, they are inherently connected to emotions about social interactions and feelings around SEEKING, CARE, PANIC, and PLAY. In Chapter 3, we will explain more about how attachment works. Here, we want to complete the explanation of how our Intuitive Brain can go from an asset to an impediment.

For the rational brain, the challenge often comes from decision-making. Our Intuitive Brain holds our memory and associative capacities. This is where our mental models fit. We are building cognitive mental models about the world based on our experience. These models are necessary for survival. They help us navigate and simplify the world around us.

In the workplace, we regularly use mental models to inform our decision-making. As mentioned above, we use analogues to sort information and speed our way to a decision. But what happens if we repeatedly use the same analogue despite the circumstances changing? In their famous study of historical analogues, *Thinking in Time*, Richard Neustadt and Earnest May demonstrate the disastrous consequences of historical examples of failed attempts to apply past analogies to current thinking. It is not that we should avoid making analogies to the past, but that we should be careful not to force information to fit the analogy of the past. This forcing is something our Intuitive Brain desires because it makes the workload a little easier.

Shawn Achor offers a strong example in his book *The Happiness Advantage*. Achor explains how the training of doctors in medical school includes a process of role-playing wherein aspiring doctors make diagnoses of imaginary patients. The PLAY proceeds with the students reviewing a set of symptoms and medical history to come to a potential diagnosis. Repeated studies of these sessions observe that students struggle to let go of their initial diagnosis in these role-playing sessions. The would-be doctors are using their mental models to form an initial diagnosis, but then the Intuitive Brain is struggling to let go of that original conclusion even as new information is presented. This mental challenge is often called "anchoring" and the initial diagnosis is known as the "anchoring point."[11]

Of course, this makes sense because the Intuitive Brain is storing years of information and training around symptoms and diagnosis that have been paired together through a series of mental models in the Limbic System that the cortical brain is just itching to connect. But then why is it hard to move from the anchoring point? What happens when something challenges these mental models? What happens when someone says, "Have you ever considered that you might be anchoring to a diagnosis?"

The challenges to these mental models feel mildly threatening. Why? Well, because our mental models are co-located with our emotions. More specifically, the social emotions including PANIC, which can be easily triggered. Our first response is one of concern for survival. Afterall, we initially created mental models to help us survive. Our second reaction is a memory of a past emotion or a similar experience, which was likely another time that we felt this very same mental model was challenged and we had to fight for survival.

WHOSE MENTAL MODEL IS IT ANYWAY?

It can be hard to change someone's mental model, but it can be even harder when you aren't sure who is really the target for change. Between 2013 and 2015, Victoria worked with teachers across a set of rural school districts on a technology initiative to revolutionize their teaching approach. These districts represented 233 schools across the United States. The goal was to deploy new technologies to help teachers bring more robust and dynamic information to their students. Her team was focused on how to get the teachers to adopt the emerging technology for productive learning.

In order to the learn the new tools, teachers were trained by technology experts on the new resources. The program included a mix of technological devices (tablets) and software (online learning, interactive programs, web conferencing) that would connect the classroom to assets way beyond the county line. However, most found they got their real training from the students that helped them once the technology experts left.

In general, the teachers were not receptive to change. On a scale of one to five (one being resistant and five being adaptive), they were mostly a two. Victoria knew, because she surveyed them … regularly. In total, her team evaluated 4,667 teachers across the school districts to determine their reaction to change. They found most of them struggled with the dramatic shift in approach to their standard way of teaching. This was a complete shift in mental model for the profession that they had been trained for and served in their entire life. Of course, eventually, most of them moved toward adoption. Even the toughest critics found their way toward adoption over time.

The really interesting part of the story comes from two districts in particular. These two districts not only adopted the new technology, but adopted the technology faster than the rest and really seemed to flourish under the approach. But why? It turns out that in these two districts, the mental model change came not just for the teachers, but for the entire community. In these two highly successful districts, there was an entire campaign across the community to introduce the technologically driven approach, discuss the program, and celebrate the success of the teachers and the school. These two communities were not just relying on the teachers to shift their mental models, the communities were shifting too. This support made it easier for the teachers to adopt the new technology and the communities move toward more effective learning.

This makes sense because we know that our Intuitive Brain handles both our memory and our emotions. Therefore, any challenge to a mental model will inherently link to our emotions and illicit an emotional reaction. In a group setting, this emotional reaction might be stronger and more pronounced because the Limbic System specifically houses the *social* emotional response. So, to return to our doctor's role-play from Shawn Achor, when a budding doctor has their potential diagnosis challenged in a group setting after years of training the challenge is hitting not just an emotional response, but an emotional response that is tied to that future doctor's entire social emotional history.

WILL THE INTUITIVE BRAIN ALWAYS BE STUCK?

We come to the workplace with a lot on our mind. Our evolutionary past brought us a complex brain with three parts that represent the instinctive, intuitive, and thoughtful components of ourselves. This is how the brain's evolution becomes central to our behavior in the workplace. Even today, as we work in organizations, we find that our work (necessary for our survival) in the economy is fundamentally linked to collaboration with others, where our emotions will be on full display. Our own limitations must be augmented by others known as our colleagues; however, we need to be able to collaborate with those colleagues to effectively do productive work.

Many organizations need employees that solve problems with their rational brains and can collaborate with their colleagues to fill the gaps they are incapable of solving themselves. But that's not the brains we have and that's not the brains we build. Our brains are designed to rely on the intuitive side first and leverage the cognitive/rational side for the more complex problems that rarely come. Our western educational systems from an early age emphasize testing that leads to rote memorization that leverages a part of the brain's design to become intuitive at the expensive of rational problem-solving. And our collaborative nature is dulled by telling our colleagues not to bring their emotional side to work. A fruitless request that is asking them to leave the very tools they need for collaboration at the door (even if it means managers must learn to deal with some of the negative consequences that come along with those very tools).

Just like Madalyn's strategy for sales, our brain has been plodding along on its path for survival. But the goals have changed. No longer does society ask us to collaborate for the hunt, it demands much more. In fact, society expects the brain to keep up with evolution. We have taken 22 million years to get the brain we have today and now we expect the same evolution every 22 milliseconds.

But there is hope. First, organizations must recognize this conflict between our pace of organizational evolution and the evolution of the brain. While it may seem like an argument for an emotionally centered workplace, it is not. In the Service Economy, we depend on our workforce to represent us to the outside world. In the Knowledge Economy, we engage our workforce to collaboratively solve problems. In the Interaction Economy, we may be leveraging someone else's assets or employees (such as Uber or AirBnB). In all three cases, people are central to the success of the organization. When people matter, the brain matters. As Jerry Colonna notes, "Certain childhood belief systems" are coming to the workplace whether we like it or not. It is really your choice whether you acknowledge them and work with them or ignore them and fight them in an uphill battle.

Second, we know the root of these challenges and we can manage them. While the brain is on a slow evolutionary path, each brain has its own challenges and individual reasons for getting Stuck. Yet, we now know where these challenges form in the brain and why. They form because our Limbic System converts our learning, emotions, and short-term memories into long-term memories that become our intuitive behavior. Once something is intuitive behavior it is viewed by the outside world as being Stuck.

But what is done can be undone. The same part of the brain that learned these intuitive behaviors is responsible for learning new behaviors. Our Limbic System can help us learn new behaviors combined with new emotions that will allow us to evolve. And through the process of long-term potentiation, our brains can make these into new intuitive behaviors. That is the biological process for becoming Unstuck. As we will discuss more in Chapter 3, it is easier said than done.

Our tortoise brains will never catch the hare. Moore's law says that we can expect our technology to become twice as fast and half as expensive every year. Some technology experts think we have outpaced this phenomenon with newer technologies. Moreover, a globalized economy running 24 hours a day with petabytes of data is a far cry from the social hunting club of 20,000 years ago. The goal should not be to keep up, but rather to help organizations give the tortoise a nudge so that we don't get Stuck along the way.

PRACTICAL EXERCISES

REFLECT: IDENTIFY YOUR MENTAL MODELS

We all use mental models to navigate the world. They are useful for reducing the amount of time we spend processing information to make decisions and react to the stimuli thrown at us.

- **Map the Decision…Backwards**: Take an important organizational decision you are about to make. Write down the full logic for the decision in the way that we tend to think about it:
  - Establish decision criteria
  - Generate alternatives
  - Evaluate alternatives
  - Select the best alternative

Then try working through the process backwards. Write the problem on the left-hand side of the page and the decision on the right hand of the page. Work backward through this process, this time focusing on the some of the unseen constraints on your decision:

- What are the potential ethical challenges associated with this decision?
- What are the organizational constraints on this decision?
- What possible biases do I bring to this decision?
- Were there options that I quickly eliminated? Why?
- Did I eliminate options because I know how they would be responded to within the organization?
- Did I eliminate options because of financial constraints?
- Did I eliminate options because of some of the other decision-makers and how they would respond to the options?
- If so, you might be identifying some of the mental models you applied to the decision.

Identify Their Mental Model: This is a way to identify mental models in yourself by focusing on mental models in others. It is a bit of game. If you can sit in your organization and listen effectively to how others are forming mental models, it may help you determine what mental models you are developing.

- Watch how others are formulating their questions.
- See how they bring together pieces of information.
- What filters do they apply?
- How often do you hear them apply analogies to past work?
- Have you ever used the same filters or the same analogies?
- If so, you are using that mental model too!

 APPLY: 10 COMMON MENTAL MODEL ERRORS

We often get Stuck repeatedly using mental models to make decisions to our own limitation. These errors come in several different forms, but some of the most common forms are in Table 2.2. What is your most common mental model error?

TABLE 2.2

Common Mental Model Errors Many of these errors were cited in an important piece from 1998: Hammond, John S.; Keeney, Ralph L.; and Raiffa, Howard. (1998). "The Hidden Traps in Decision Making." *Harvard Business Review*, Sept-Oct 1998.

Confirming Evidence	We tend to look for reasons to support what we would like to happen
Sunk Cost	We tend to make choices in a way that justifies past choices and past resource commitment
Status Quo	We tend to favor decisions that perpetuate what is already happening
Anchoring	We give disproportionate weight to the first information we receive
Overconfidence	We tend to believe strongly in the accuracy of our predictions
Framing	We make our choice based on the way the problem is set up for us
Gain Framing	We are risk-averse when the issue is framed in terms of what we may gain from a situation
Loss Framing	We are risk-seeking when the issue is framed in terms of what we may lose from a situation
Reference Point Framing	We shift the point of orientation to evoke different possible outcomes
Implicit Bias	We have underlying factors or assumptions that skew our viewpoints of a subject

 APPLY: YOUR EMOTIONAL PROFILE

We use emotional traps just like mental models. The emotional traps speak to our personality and how others view us in the workplace. Dr. John Gottman evolved Jaak Panksepp's seven emotional systems into a set of personas. Undoubtedly, as you read the seven emotional systems you could not help but think about how these might apply to you and the people around you. In truth, no one system dominates a single person, but Gottman's approach allows for an understanding of these roles at the extremes (both overuse and under use) in a personified form.

- **Jester:** The one who emphasizes the fun and PLAY in life by pursuing leisure and recreation over all else. Too much use of this persona can lead to silliness; too little can lead to lethargy and ultimately challenges like depression.

- **Sensualist:** The core characteristics of this persona are attraction and LUST. Too much of this character could lead to sexual risk-taking and challenges in the workplace like sexual harassment. Too little use of this persona leads to aversion and depression.
- **Nest-Builder:** A persona that desires affiliation and CARE from others. Both an over activation and under activation of this character can lead to anxiety – with a loss of personal boundaries when over activated and a sense of loss when under activated.
- **Commander-in-Chief:** A controlling persona that works through power and can lead to aggression and RAGE. The right balance here will demonstrate confidence. However, too much of the persona quickly leads to anger and too little will quickly dissipate to passivity and frustration.
- **Explorer:** A persona that is SEEKING for answers and new experiences with goal setting and curiosity. Too much of this persona can lead to obsessive behavior and overwork, while too little can lead to boredom and restlessness.
- **Energy Czar:** A health-conscious persona on the surface that might be governing their own concerns of PANIC. With balance, this persona manages energy effectively with good balance of exercise, diet, and relaxation. However, the same overactive behaviors might lead to shame and guilt; while underactive versions of the persona might lead to fatigue, weakened immunity, and depression.
- **Sentry:** This persona is always on guard and can be quite FEARful of the world around. Over activation of this character can lead to phobias and paranoia, while an under activation can lead to carelessness and risk-taking.

Possible Group Activity:

Act Them Inside Out. Disney Pixar's 2015 film *Inside Out* tells the story of how our emotions work together to govern the body of one growing girl, Riley. We watch as Riley's personified emotions react (in their own way) to major changes in her life. If you want to help your colleagues understand how these different emotions influence the workplace and support perspective taking, do some role-playing with your colleagues. Try bringing the emotions from the Inside…Out.

Pick a common setting at work and ask your team members to play the seven different emotional systems as you discuss a common organizational challenge. This could be a light topic as a form of team building or it could be a light approach to break through on wicked problem the team has been struggling to address.

Note: be careful who you select for the Sensualist! This one should not be overplayed!

NOTES

1   Ainsworth, M. (1989). "Attachments Beyond Infancy." *American Psychologist*, 44(4), p. 713.

2   Wilson, E. O. (2012). *The Social Conquest of Earth*. New York: W.W. Norton & Company, pp. 178–180.

3   Bryson, B. (2004). *A Short History of Nearly Everything*. New York: Broadway Books.
    Diamond, J. (2013). *The World Until Yesterday: What Can We Learn From Traditional Societies?* New York: Penguin.
    Fagan, B. (2011). *Cro-Magnon: How the Ice Age Gave Birth to the First Modern Humans*. New York: Bloomsbury Press.
    Lachmann, P. (2010). Genetic and Cultural Evolution: From Fossils to Proteins, and from Behaviour to Ethics. *European Review*, 18(3), 297–309. doi:http://dx.doi.org.library.capella.edu/10.1017/S1062798710000050 Tattersall, I. (2012). *Masters of the Planet: The Search for Our Human Origins*. New York: St. Martin's Press.

4   Achor, S. (2010). *The Happiness Advantage: The Seven Principles of Positive Psychology That Fuel Success and Performance at Work*. New York: Currency, pp. 147–148.

5   Bowlby, J. (1969). *Attachment and Loss, vol. 1: Attachment*. New York: Basic Books, pp. 61–62.

6   MacLean, Paul D. (1990). *The Triune Brain in Evolution: Role in Paleocerebral Functions*. New York: Plenum Press.

7   Kahneman, Daniel. (2003). "Maps of Bounded Rationality: Psychology for Behavioral Economics." *The American Economic Review*, 93(5), pp. 1449–1475.

8   Kahneman, D. (2003). "Maps of Bounded Rationality: Psychology for Behavioral Economics." *The American Economic Review*, 93(5), pp. 1449–1475.

9   Grady, J., Grady, V., McCreesh, P., and Noakes, I. (2020). *Workplace Attachments: Managing Beneath the Surface*. New York: Routledge, p. 43. Cozolino, L. (2014). *The*

Neuroscience of Human Relationships: Attachment and the Developing Social Brain (2nd ed.). New York: W. W. Norton & Company.

10 Panksepp, J. (1998). *Affective Neuroscience: The Foundations of Human and Animal Emotions.* New York: Oxford University Press, Inc.

11 Achor, S. (2010). *The Happiness Advantage: The Seven Principles of Positive Psychology That Fuel Success and Performance at Work.* New York: Currency, p. 47.

3

Why Do I Get Stuck?

"Attachment ... is the result of the activity of behavioral systems that have a continuing set goal, that of maintaining a specified relationship."

John Bowlby[1]

"[There is] ... a particular circumscribed form of melancholia that we often experience when individuals, organizations, or belief systems that we lean on or are dependent on for emotional support are withdrawn from us."

Jerry Harvey[2]

"No one ever told me that grief felt so like fear."

C.S. Lewis

Jenna moved to Washington, DC in October of 2018 after finishing graduate school. She was like many of the people who joined her consulting company – she was new to the company, new to the industry, and new to the area. On her first day of orientation, she was introduced to Joshua. They had a lot in common. They shared similar views on the world, they were both from New Jersey, they both left home for college and grad school, and they were both in serious relationships with people that were "back home."

Over the next few days of orientation Jenna and Joshua formed a quick bond – they joked about the exercises together and continued to learn more about each other. As the orientation was ending, they assumed they would find their roles and would separate into the massive 20,000 person company with just email to connect them. Instead, Jenna was relieved to learn that they were assigned to the same team and the same first project. This would allow them to continue to build their friendship over the first few tenuous months of a new company.

DOI: 10.4324/9781003157458-3

By the spring of 2019, Jenna and Joshua were inseparable. They walked to the client site every day together, they hosted regular happy hours for their project team together, they went to the gym together, and they made plans to take the train home to New Jersey on the weekends together. In the summer, Joshua got engaged and Jenna was elated. In the fall, Jenna was promoted based in good measure on Joshua's personal write-up of all her efforts at work. They supported each other as both colleagues and friends.

On March 16, 2020, over 48 million Americans attempted to do something new at the same time – work from home due to the COVID 19 pandemic.[3] Jenna and Joshua rented a car and drove back to New Jersey. They settled in with their respective significant others and hunkered down for the next year. There were no more happy hours. No more workouts. They did not share a workspace for 13 months.

Yet, every morning they got on Zoom and started working together. Over time, Joshua and his fiancé decided to have a private wedding during the pandemic. Jenna and her boyfriend got engaged. Joshua was promoted based on the recommendation of Jenna and was to move to a new role in New York following the pandemic. Meanwhile, Jenna and her fiancé jointly relocated back to DC in the spring of 2021. Even though they both were building families elsewhere, Jenna and Joshua stayed strongly connected to each other.

They also stayed connected to the company. They continued to share playful jokes about things going on in the company and they commiserated about work virtually over wine. Both were asked to move into managerial roles, and they talked regularly to share the experience and compare notes. In the spring of 2021, Jenna was approached with a job offer from an up-and-coming small business where she would have a bigger role that included 25 percent more money, better benefits, and the opportunity for equity in the company. She rejected the offer and when asked why by the recruiter making the offer, she simply said, "I have a good social network here."

Jenna was entering her third year with a company where she had spent most of that time in a virtual setting due to the pandemic. How could Jenna possibly have a social network at that company? She was being offered more money, more benefits, and more visibility. Why would she be so Stuck on her current role? Maybe it doesn't have anything to do with her company per se, maybe it is about something else.

From another angle, Jenna moved to a new town where she didn't know anyone and she didn't develop a career, she developed a friendship. That friendship is what she was connected to at the company. While she may have found other attractive elements of the company that she could say she appreciated, it was the friendship with Joshua that had sustained her through a tough transition to Washington, DC, a pandemic year, and all the late nights of work. When she thought of the company, she didn't see the logo, she saw Joshua.

Attachment is the Human Need to Lean on Tangible and/or Intangible Objects for Support

The definition is simple. The concept is not. **Attachment** is biological and builds from the Intuitive Brain we explored in Chapter 2. This means that attachment is not simply a preference for something. Attachment is instinctual. Attachments form in the limbic system through a mix of memory, emotion, and learning.

Let's skip ahead...attachment to what? The **tangible** and **intangible objects** can truly be anything around us. The tangible might be people, places, or things. We connect with people and talk to them about our problems, but we also can be comforted by just knowing they are present. Likewise, we can be comforted in certain places or with certain objects, whether it is the presence of our *"lucky penny"* or just having our Red Swingline (like Milton from the movie Office Space). The intangible objects are the ideas that we lean on for support. The concepts in our groups, organizations, communities, and countries that connect us to the larger set of people around us. These ideas might be as abstract as mission statements or they might be more enforceable like written laws. Either way, we attach to these intangible ideas.

The human need to lean on objects for support. We all need support throughout our lifetime of social interactions. As Chapter 2 showed us, the evolutionary process helped us become socially interacting beings with a dependence on each other, but that doesn't mean it comes naturally. We still have a SEEKING function to find support that helps us through our daily lives. We seek that connection in all settings of our lives, including the workplace. When that connection is removed, we get Stuck.

We have an unwillingness to let go of the object. It is a sense of loss due to the nature of the attachment and the depth of the connection. The depth of the connection is a direct result of the importance of that attachment. In a mild form, this sense of loss is as if something has been borrowed from us. In a deeper form, such as the loss of a loved one, it comes with the appropriate grief and fear that comes following a death. For some people, attachments form that yield a sense of loss as great as losing someone even if it is not as severe an actual loss.

In this chapter we will explore:

- How does the brain get Stuck?
- How does it connect to biology?
- What is attachment and how does it develop?
- What are some of the ways we get Stuck at work?

THE ROOTS OF ATTACHMENT

We get Stuck in the brain. Attachment is rooted in the Intuitive Brain (the Limbic System), where memory, emotion, and learning come together to coalesce around past connections. Attachment is a concept that starts early in our lives. In fact, it starts at birth. In our early days of life, we have a connection to our original caretaker, and we form an attachment. There is certainly a physical dependency on this person for basic needs of food and cleanliness. However, a deeper connection is also forming. If we think back to Chapter 2, our Intuitive Brain is building in the memory-emotion-learning core how to develop the social interactions and emotions around a single person. These feelings are a combination of the emotions around SEEKING, CARE, PANIC, and PLAY.

A newborn child is slowly but surely developing these social-emotional feelings. The SEEKING is the basic human desire to find those for interaction, which starts from birth. CARE is what is the tenderness and love that is both provided and sought, which builds the formation between the infant version of ourselves and the early caretaker. PLAY is the positive response that emerges as we understand that we receive enjoyment from active interactions with others. Last, PANIC is what the infant finds when the caretaker is missing, even for a brief period. What the child feels is a real sense of loss for the missing caretaker. As John Bowlby notes,

> whenever a young child who has the opportunity to develop an attachment to a mother figure is separated from her ... he behaves in a typical sequence ... first he protests ... later he seems to despair ... [and finally] he seems to become detached.[4]

A BABY AT A PARTY: SEPARATION ANXIETY OR HEALTHY ATTACHMENT?

If you think of your observations of infants, you have probably seen all these behaviors. Just imagine a six-month-old that comes to your house during a party. The child comes into your home in their parents' arms. Hesitantly, the young child clings to their parent, sometimes seemingly climbing up their father's coat or their mother's sweater. What are they SEEKING? They just want the known CARE and comfort from their caretaker. Over time, you or one of the other people in your home might take out a small toy that introduces PLAY. The child recognizes it as similar to the same PLAY they have with their parents. In fact, they look back at their parents to confirm it is the *PLAY* they know. The child will PLAY for a while and even forget about their parent. Then they look up and notice that mom or dad went for a cup of coffee and they lose their mind. PANIC sets in. The child goes back to SEEKING and finds the caretaker they know provides CARE and comfort.

We are quick to call this separation anxiety. While this may be an appropriate clinical terminology for what is happening, it is at once oversimplifying and providing a negative context to an affective process. As we just saw, there were many positives to the relationship that the child formed with the parent that made it possible for a six-month-old to come into a new home and interact with a new person. The child looks to the parent for reinforcement of the social norms and even accepts that the new situation must be acceptable based on the parent's comfort. These are positives of the relationship.

The oversimplification is that the child does not just miss the parent, the child does not know if the parent will come back. When the caretaker goes missing the child lacks the understanding of object permanence to know the parent will be back. Additionally, we over-simplify with the term "anxiety" because the PANIC emotion as a social emotion is more often associated with guilt. This means the child may think they *caused* the parent to leave ... forever. Now, that's daunting for a six-month-old. Over time, the child will have a series of situations where the parent leaves and comes back, which will reinforce the memory function of the Limbic System to coordinate with the emotional systems to understand that the separation is temporary. Even in the healthiest of attachments, the child will still feel a sense of PANIC when the parent leaves, but the intensity will dissipate, and the child will learn to regulate the emotion.

What's happening in our brain through the attachment process? We previously mentioned long-term potentiation (LTP). This is how the brain physiologically forms attachments, but to understand attachments, we must understand how they form in our brain. Attachments are instinctual and evolve as a combination of memory and emotion. In this way, they are incredibly powerful because they work in the Intuitive Brain where all the social emotional functions reside. Therefore, they are inherently connected to emotions about social interactions and feelings around SEEKING, CARE, PANIC, and PLAY.

Attachment is, in short, a hard-wired mental model. It resides in the same place as other mental models in the Intuitive Brain (the Limbic System) and it is formed through the same combination of memory, emotion, and learning. Like other mental models, it is formed in the early days of life. The key difference from other mental models is that it lacks an algorithmic element to it. It is purely biological. There is little ability for the body to apply it like some of the decision-based criteria in Chapter 2. The attachment mental model in adults sits in the intuitive brain where the emotions become learned and reinforced by memory. It becomes a biological response.

Throughout our lives, we move away from these original caretakers both physically and emotionally, we attach to others and find new anchors. These emotions can develop effective attachment characteristics for children. Children come to develop a healthy dependence on parents and caretakers for their physical and psychological needs. We lean on these caretakers through our youth and developmentally difficult teenage years as the anchors to provide stability and remind us of our original comfort. As this happens, we always attempt to connect these new attachments via the same social-emotional systems – SEEKING, CARE, PANIC, and PLAY – and as a result know we always feel a sense of loss when one of these attachments ends. However, with effective attachment behavior, this sense of loss is managed and recovered effectively.

Objects play a critical role in the attachment process. They are both the source of attachment (in the form of the initial caretaker) and they help people regulate their emotions through the period of loss when an attachment is broken. This is why the definition of attachment includes this element of "lean on ... objects." At the beginning of life, these objects include things like blankets and binkys (often a playful term for pacifiers). Young children lean on these objects for support in separation from their parents or caretakers. As they grow up, the objects may turn into teddy bears or other beloved stuffed animals. For others, different behaviors may develop that serve as the comfort mechanism, such thumb sucking or nail-biting as a young child. These different forms of comfort mechanisms will yield different types of attachment behavior throughout adult life.

Throughout life, we can transition, almost like moving across monkey bars, from one object of support to another when we have an effective and secure base of attachment. Of course, we can also develop ineffective attachment behavior. As noted in Chapter 2, all emotional systems have both negatives and extremes. Elements of detachment can lead to guilt, shame, anxiety, or worse, depression. As we grow into adults, we likely don't feel the same intensity of separation from our earliest attachments that we did when we were infants, but we do take some lasting tendencies with us. Two important things are formed in these early days of life: (1) how we attach and respond to loss (Attachment Styles in Chapter 4) and (2) our Attachment Objects (Chapter 5).

Regardless of both factors (Attachment Styles and Attachment Objects), a sense of loss can happen for anyone. It is the intensity of the loss, the emotional regulation around the loss, and the response that will vary based on the Attachment Object and the Attachment Style. For example, the loss of a loved one should be hard for everyone. No exceptions. For a teenager, not getting into your top-choice school may vary based on the root of the attachment (connection to the school) and the way the person attaches to the situation (the attachment style).

ADULT ATTACHMENT

The characteristics of attachment continue into our adult life. The idea of attachment behavior in adults is most attributed to Mary Ainsworth and John Bowlby. The two developmental psychologists, she American and he British, provided a wealth of research between 1960 and 1990 on the topics of child development and attachment, even collaborating on early books about childcare. Separately and together, they pulled the thread from childhood to adult.

Much of Ainsworth's research focused on the individual.[5] She sought to identify the relationship that led to the attachment bonds in early children and how the nature-nurture paradigm impacted children. Bowlby studied the exact same attachment concept, but from a slightly different angle. He focused more on the social impacts of attachment and the role of attachment issues in group behavior. For this reason, when we look at the workplace, we will focus a little more on Bowlby.

As noted in the quotation at the outset of this chapter, Bowlby summarized attachment behavior as crucial for "maintaining a specified relationship."[6] As he evolved his research, he went on to note that as adults grow into effective individuals with healthy attachments they will develop a healthy response to loss, which he defines as

> the successful effort of an individual to accept both that a change has occurred in his external world and that he is required to make corresponding changes in his internal, representational, world and to reorganize, and perhaps to reorient, his attachment behavior accordingly.[7]

Bowlby developed an overarching view of attachment behavior that he characterized as:

- Attachment behavior is conceived as being a distinct form of behavior and is equivalent to those other forms of instinctual behavior that enhance survival.

- Attachment behavior in healthy development leads to affectional bonds, initially between a child and parent and later between an adult and another adult.
- The goal of attachment behavior is to maintain proximity to or connections with the preferred attachment figure.
- Very intense emotions are involved during the formation, maintenance, disruption, and/or renewal of attachment relationships.
- Attachment behavior contributes to individual and species survival.
- Attachment behavior is potentially active throughout life, and when active in an adult it is not an indication of pathology or regression.

In this last bullet, Bowlby offers that attachment is "potentially active throughout life." As Judith Crowell et al. note, "Although Bowlby and Ainsworth clearly acknowledged the importance of the attachment system across the lifespan, they provide relatively few guidelines concerning its specific function and expression later in life."[8] Subsequent work by several researchers provides superior guidance in the application of attachment behavior to adults and evidence of attachment behavior in adults.[9] We have collectively published extensively our own research findings on attachment behavior in adults across organizations of all types around the world.[10]

Whether we like it or not, our reaction to loss as adults is not that biologically different from that baby at a party. When a very young child cannot find a parent, it triggers the mechanism called Anaclitic Depression, which we tend to call Separation Anxiety. When the child cannot find the primary caretaker, the emotional side of the Intuitive Brain takes over involving "excessive interpersonal concerns, including feelings of loneliness, weakness, helplessness and abandonment fears."[11] The same is true for an adult. When an adult loses an attachment of value, we will show observable symptoms of these feelings of loss that mirror the Executive Emotional Systems we explored in Chapter 2[12]:

Symptoms in the Individual

- Frustration
- Apprehension (Anxiety)
- Rejection of the Environment

- Withdrawal
- Refusal to Participate
- Delayed Development

Imagine an adult loses his phone. He may be frustrated. He may be a little anxious. He may refuse to be a part of the meeting until he can find his phone. He may ask his colleagues if they have seen it. He may not do any work at all until he can find his phone. No, he may need to take off the rest of the day to go and find his phone. All this while his open computer sits in front of him with much the same functionality. Why? Because it is *his* phone. That object matters. We have all seen it before and it demonstrates how these symptoms can play out for an individual that has lost an object of importance.

The adult begins SEEKING a primary attachment response for the object. This is a comfort center that is the type of comfort they sought as a child. Just like the child SEEKING a comfort object, adults can be calmed using objects. These objects may evolve over time and they will vary. Some adults are comforted by people and some are comforted by physical objects. Some are comforted by processes or information.

Imagine a different scenario where a woman loses her phone. A colleague immediately realizes her PANIC and decides to support her. The colleague calls her phone. It is not ringing, but together they try an app from her computer to find the phone. That does not work, but they agree that after the meeting they will look together and perhaps contact the cell company about the pre-paid insurance to get a new phone. Because there was a comforting object walking her through her responses, she did not devolve into frustration, reject the environment, or do herself a professional disservice. In short, the introduction of a comforting object helped her regulate her emotional systems in a time of a loss.

GETTING STUCK AT WORK?

By now, we hope the connection of these concepts to the workplace is apparent. If adults have attachment behaviors, we also bring them to work. We may want to pretend that our behavior is rational in the moment, that we cross some imaginary threshold from home to work, but it simply does not happen. Instead, the Intuitive Brain and our attachment behavior moves with us through the doorway where we enter the working world. What comes with it is our set of attachments formed by our earliest days of life. It reveals itself in our daily work through simple things like our daily habits and our interactions with team members. In the late 1980s, research began to move beyond intimate relationships and demonstrate a strong connection of attachment with the challenges of everyday life. It is only over the last 20 years that the pace of dedicated research on attachment in the workplace has significantly quickened.[13]

Additionally, the growing popular literature around habit formation hits on the importance of attachment behavior. Habits are simply a repeated practice or routine. In 1989, Stephen Covey's #1 National Bestseller *The 7 Habits of Highly Effective People* defines a habit as the intersection of knowledge, skill, and desire.

> Knowledge is the theoretical paradigm, the *what* to do and the *why*. Skill is the *how* to do. And desire is the motivation, the *want* to do. In order to make something a habit in our lives, we have to have all three.[14]

Creating a desire is about getting ourselves in a position where we are either willing to break an existing mental model or establish a new mental model. For this, there must be an emotional connection with the purpose of creating the new habit long enough for the mental model to Stick.

Of course, the flip side of getting a new habit to Stick is when we get Stuck. This is often called resistance. Resistance is a real challenge in organizations, but as we will discuss at a few points in this book, sometimes resistance is rational. Even more often, resistance is the attachment symptoms of the individual coming out in response to a perceived or actual change. The person is Stuck. The organization decides to make a change to one of the very elements that the employee grew to lean on for support in their daily work – a system, a process, a person, or an idea. Now, instead of freely giving up that item, the team members' reaction is to dig in and say "No, I will not change."

Under the surface, that person is really feeling the symptoms of attachment. As Dr. Jerry Harvey notes, the same attachment mechanism carries over from adult life into the work world:

> Being abandoned by, ostracized by, or separated from individuals whom we know and lean on is an experience that frequently has a devastating impact

on our lives. Likewise, being ostracized by, separated from, or abandoned by cherished organizations, many of whose members we may not know personally can generate the anaclitic depression blues.[15]

Our team member is frustrated that she is being asked to do something new, work with someone new, or use a new system. She is a little nervous about it. She may withdraw from her work and she may (initially) step back from participation. This will hinder her ability to grow and advance. In short, she will resist. It may not be logical. In fact, it may be counter to her own interests, but if she is feeling like something will be lost; it is biological.

In the book *Switch,* the Heath Brothers (Chip and Dan) describe the brain via a parable of two parts, involving a rider on an elephant. The rider represents our rational side that can see what is happening in the world around us and understands logically what to do to change. The elephant represents the emotional side, the intuitive brain, that gets Stuck. The Heath Brothers also note the need for an emotional connection to "Motivate the Elephant" by "Finding the Feeling" to move the individual in the right direction. As they explain, only when you bring together the logical and rational rider with the intuitive and emotional elephant can you "Build Habits" that will lead to the new behavior sought by the organization.[16]

This is both the power and the challenge of getting Stuck. We want to develop our workplace to leverage the Intuitive Brain to support our team members and employees in an organization. We want them to build the effective habits of the organization that will drive support individual development and growth while supporting organizational productivity, *but* we don't want that emotional side to get Stuck. We want the emotional side to remain flexible enough to be re-engaged and motivated in a new direction if the organization needs to move in a different direction. For each person, that is a complicated dance. It requires attachment to a set of core elements that remain constant while many things around the person may change. It is like tying one's attachments to a drainpipe while a tornado happens around you. It's like finding a Joshua.

As we learned in Chapter 2, we come to work with a brain that is focused on survival first and we use mental models to support our way through the world. In this chapter, we found that attachment is like one of those mental models, but more powerful. Attachment is not based on logic and reason to help us physically navigate the world, but rather emotions and memory.

The attachment process is co-located in Limbic System of the Intuitive Brain where it is connected to our emotional systems and our response to situations that challenge our attachments will be reactive, biological, and emotional. These reactions will demonstrate the symptoms of loss.

And yet, we have all found ways to navigate through the world and regulate these emotional processes. We can never replace our first caretaker, but we can lean on objects throughout our life to support us. These objects serve as proxies to help us regulate our emotions. Through different attachment objects, we can manage our emotional systems and effectively regulate the unending process of change that happens around us. Each of us has a different way of regulating these emotional processes called attachment styles. We will explore these in the next chapter. It is the combination of our unique attachment style and attachment objects (Chapter 5) that determine how we behave in the workplace and how often we get Stuck.

PRACTICAL EXERCISES

 REFLECT: IDENTIFYING MEL AND MELANIE

Attachment starts a birth and is a constant process of connecting and reconnecting throughout life. To understand our attachments a little better, it is important to understand some of our early attachments. These Stick in the Intuitive Brain where Memory, Emotion, and Learning come together. An easy pneumonic device to remember this concept is M E L. So, a way to think about this for you is to think about identifying your MEL or MELanie.

The following questions are designed to help you think about your MEL or MELanie – what attachments formed in your youth and how these may, or may not, influence you today:

- Who is the first person you remember caring for you as a child?
  - How do you think about this person?
  - Do you think about them favorably? Negatively?
  - Do you ever compare people in your life to this person?
  - If so, how do you ever explain this connection to the person? Do they understand why you view them this way?

- What is the first object you remember being "yours" as a child?
  - What did it look like?
  - How old were you when you got it?
  - Who gave it to you?
  - How long did you have it?
  - Where is it now?
- Do you remember the first time that you felt lost – meaning you didn't know where you were, or you lost track of a parent/caretaker in a public setting?
  - How did you feel in that situation?
  - How did you ultimately resolve the situation?
  - Have you ever thought about that moment again?
- Who is the first person close to you that you remember losing to death?
  - How did this person shape your life?
  - How often do you think about this person now?
  - Do you think about this person when others talk about losing someone they care about?
  - Does anyone that you work with remind you of this person?

As you work through these reflections, you will find a set of early memories that will serve as the core of your attachments today. The purpose is to get you thinking about how these earliest memories may influence who and what you lean on for support today.

  COLLECT AND ANALYZE: HABITS GET STUCK

As we discussed in this chapter, habit formation happens in a very similar way to the attachment process. Habits are often described as a positive, whereas attachments can have a negative connotation. Let's see if we can find some of the habits that we have (both positive and negative) that we can work with to help us understand our own attachments.

In a chart like Table 3.1, list out your daily habits. These could be things at home like drinking coffee or walking the dog, or it could

TABLE 3.1

Habit Tracker

Habit	Good for me?	Good for others?	Good for org?	Bad for me?	Bad for others?	Bad for org?

be more complicated work activities like uploading certain files or tracking time. The point is just to track some of your daily habits. Those things you do every day. Then, look at that list and think about whyyou do them and who they serve. Are the habits good for you, another person, or the organization? Or are they bad for you, another person, or the organization?

Upon reviewing these habits, are any of these habits worth changing? What would it take to do that?

 REFLECT: SOMETHING CHANGED, PART 2

At the end of Chapter 1, we asked you to write down an example of a change at work. Take a moment to go back and read the notes you wrote down.

It's okay, we will wait.

Now, thinking again about that change, did you or others have a negative reaction to the change? Based on the content of this chapter, do you think it is possible you or others felt any sort of loss during that period of your life?

Was there some aspect of the change that took away something from you or others at work that you valued?

If so, what do you think was taken away?

Was it a physical or an intangible object?

If you were the one who felt the loss, which of the following best represents how you felt:

- Frustration
- Apprehension
- Rejection of the Environment
- Withdrawal
- Refusal to Participate
- Delayed Development

Can you remember other times you felt this way?

NOTES

1 Bowlby, J. (1969). *Attachment and Loss, vol. 1: Attachment.* New York: Basic Books, p. 140.

2 Harvey, J. (1999). *How Come Every Time I Get Stabbed in the Back My Fingerprints Are on the Knife?* San Fransisco: Jossey-Bass, pp. 112–113.

3 "Labor Force Statistic from the Current Population Survey." Bureau of Labor Statistics. Accessed electronically on June 4, 2021 at: www.bls.gov/cps/effects-of-the-coronavirus-covid-19-pandemic.htm#concepts.

4 Bowbly, J. (1973). *Attachment and Loss, vol. 2: Separation.* New York: Basic Books, p. 26.

5 Ainsworth, M. D. S. (1989). "Attachments Beyond Infancy." *American Psychologist*, 44(4), pp. 709–716.
   Ainsworth, M. D. S. and Bell, S. M. (1970). "Attachment, Exploration, and Separation: Illustrated by the Behavior of One-Year Olds in a Strange Situation." *Child Development*, 41, pp. 49–67.
   Ainsworth, M. D. S., Bell, S. M., and Stayton, D. J. (1971). "Individual Differences in Strange-Situation Behavior of One-Year Olds." In H. R. Schaffer (Ed.), *The Origins of Human Social Relations*. London and New York: Academic Press, pp. 17–58.
   Ainsworth, M. D. S., Blehar, M. C., Waters, E., and Wall, S. (1978). *Patterns of Attachment: A Psychological Study of the Strange Situation*. Hillsdale, NJ: Erlbaum.

6 Bowlby, J. (1969). *Attachment and Loss, vol. 1: Attachment.* New York: Basic Books, p. 140.

7 Bowlby, J. (1980). *Attachment and Loss, vol. 3: Loss.* New York: Basic Books, p. 18.

8 Crowell, J., Fraley, R., and Shaver, P. (2008). "Measurement of Individual Differences in Adolescent and Adult Attachment." In J. Cassidy and P. Shaver (Eds.), *Handbook of Attachment* (2nd ed.). New York: Guilford Press, pp. 599–634.

9 Winnicott, D. (1971). *Playing and Reality.* New York: Basic Books.
   Spitz, R. and Wolf, K. (1946). "Anaclitic Depression: An Inquiry into the Genesis of Psychiatric Conditions in Early Childhood, II." *The Psychoanalytic Study of the Child*, 2, pp. 313–342.

Harvey, J. (1999). *How Come Every Time I Get Stabbed in the Back My Fingerprints Are on the Knife?: And Other Meditations on Management.* San Francisco: Jossey-Bass.

Noer, D. (1993). *Healing the Wounds: Overcoming the Trauma of Layoffs and Revitalizing Downsized Organizations.* San Fransisco: Jossey-Bass.

10 Grady, V. and Grady, J. (2008). "Winnicott's Potential Space and Tranisitional Objects: Implications for the Organizational Change Process and Its Previously Defined Relationship to an Organizational LOE." *Journal of Organizational and Social Dynamics, 8*(2), pp. 278–297.

Grady, V. and Grady, J. (2012). "The Relationship of Bowlby's Attachment Theory to the Persistent Failure of Organizational Change Initiatives." *Journal of Change Management, 13*(2), 206–222.

Grady, V. and Grady, J. (2013). *The Pivot Point: Success in Organizational Change.* New York: Morgan James.

11 Grenyer, B. and Reis, S. (2002). "Pathways to Anaclitic and Introjective Depression." *Psychology and Psychotherapy, 75*(4), pp. 445–459.

12 Grady, J., Grady, V., McCreesh, P. and Noakes, I. (2020). *Workplace Attachments: Managing Beneath the Surface.* New York: Routledge, p. 50.

13 Albert, L. S., Allen, D. G., Biggane, J. E. and Ma, Q. K. (2015). "Attachment and Responses to Employment Dissolution." *Human Resource Management Review, 25*(1), pp. 94–106.

Albert, L. S., and Horowitz, L. M. (2009). "Attachment Styles and Ethical Behavior: Their Relationship and Significance in the Marketplace." *Journal of Business Ethics, 87*(3), pp. 299–316.

Geller, D. and Bamberger, P. (2009). "Bringing Avoidance and Anxiety to the Job: Attachment Style and Instrumental Helping Behavior among Co-workers." *Human Relations, 62*(12), pp. 1803–1827.

Harms, P. D. (2011). "Adult Attachment Styles in the Workplace." *Human Resource Management Review, 21*, pp. 285–296.

14 Covey, S. (1989). *Seven Habits of Highly Effective People: Restoring the Character Ethic.* New York: Simon & Schuster, p. 47.

15 Harvey, J. (1999). *How Come Every Time I Get Stabbed in the Back My Fingerprints Are on the Knife?* San Fransisco: Jossey-Bass, p. 122.

16 Heath, C. and Heath, D. (2010). *Switch: How to Change Things When Change is Hard.* New York: Crown Business.

4

How Do I Get Stuck?

"Every human is like all other humans, some other humans, and no other human."

Clyde Kluckhohn

"It is not what happens to us, but our response to what happens to us that hurts us."

Stephen R. Covey

Venetia Reyes was the employee engagement and communications manager for Genentech Inc., a 10,000-person biotechnology division of the pharmaceutical multinational Roche. Genentech has a long history in the field of biotechnology and is consistently named one of the best places to work by *Fortune*. Between 2017 and 2018, Venetia was charged with rolling out multiple change initiatives related to business process and structure. She wanted to understand the cohort of people she would ask to change. Venetia wanted to know who they were, how would they would receive the change, how they might react, and what she could do to support them through the change.

Venetia used a tool called the Attachment Styles Index (ASI) to understand her team. This unique tool is designed around the concepts of attachment and focuses on how each person may react to a sense of loss. The tool helps identify each person's attachment style and explain how these styles may react to change. Venetia deployed the ASI with quantitative and qualitative questions and collected anonymous responses. The goal was to effectively understand the team, to design the change management strategy, and then align the structure and communications to the strategy for the effort.

DOI: 10.4324/9781003157458-4

Overall, the cohort of Genentech employees impacted by the change were eager to provide data to better inform the change process. The employees were generally highly motivated and focused on all opportunities to pro-actively create an atmosphere responsive to change, consistent with their deep commitment to organizational values. The team was excited to inte-grate a forward focused tool that was consistent with the innovative focus at Genentech. Across the across the group that was studied 73 percent of the respondents were securely attached in Genentech. Furthermore, we found that there was little variance in score over tenure, meaning that Venetia's most junior and most senior employees shared a healthy, Stable attachment style (more later on what this means).

Genentech was one of the first companies to develop biotechnology harnessing the power of DNA. This is what excited employees to come to work and may have even been the foundation of employee attachment to Genentech and the mission. Venetia and her team harnessed this connection to history and her own team's Stable attachment to this legacy to create a culture ready for change. The ASI helped Venetia design a change man-agement strategy that aligned the messaging to the mission and mitigated the challenges and potential disruption. The team was focused on how the change would help get them back to the mission of developing innovative medicines to improve the overall health of the world.

As we saw in the previous chapter, our experiences lead us to very different understandings of attachment. Our early interactions with parents and caretakers certainly impact how we develop, but this also evolves over our lifetime through other experiences. This evolution leads us to develop our own type of attachment. These are called **attachment styles**. "Attachment style is defined as an individual's patterns of expectations, needs, emotions, and social behavior that result from a particular history of attachment experiences, usually beginning in relationship with parents."[1]

The attachment style is not a personality type, but our attachment style sits underneath our personal attributes and explains some important parts of our personality. Our style does not determine how we respond to every situation in the workplace, but it is a strong signal for how we will respond to many situations. And our attachment style does not determine how we will work with our fellow team members, but it is a strong predictor of how we will interact with colleagues. Therefore, our attachment styles set the base from which many of the common organizational assessments and managerial challenges stem.

In this chapter we will explore:

- How do we Stick differently through different attachment styles?
- How do we identify our attachment style?
- What is the impact of an attachment style on you?
- How does your attachment style impact the way you show up at work?

ATTACHMENT STYLES

Attachment styles are the visible signals of the lifelong developmental experience that each person has with relationships.[2] Our first interactions with caretakers set the stage for this style. These experiences can set what is referred to as a "secure base." This would be a healthy attachment with a caretaker that is managed in a healthy way toward separation and individual development. Over time, this initial secure base is reinforced with more positive relationships that reinforce the construct toward a secure attachment style through life. Alternatively, even a secure base may be consistently challenged at a young developmental age, which would undercut the base and create different tendencies.

It is important to go back to our chapter on the brain and understand how this style is formed biologically. During the developmental process, the Intuitive Brain (the Limbic System) is writing the emotional experiences encoded with memory, almost like a Rosetta Stone, for future reference. The early experiences of a secure base are being hard wired into us as learned positive feelings – warmth, comfort, protection, safety. As these are reinforced with other positive developmental experiences like academic, athletic, or community support – care, growth, belonging.

These secure feelings stay with us via our Intuitive Brain through our working life and we feel it through professional support – respect, opportunity, development, growth. When we see someone, who demonstrates these feelings back in the workplace we tend to use a casual lexicon. Sometimes, we call the person secure, but more often we may think of some of the traits we see. We may call them confident or social.

The flip side of this secure base is an insecure base. Perhaps a person did not have a healthy separation from an initial caretaker, leaving some negative feelings – longing, concern, loss. As the person grows, these emotions, written into the Intuitive Brain, are reinforced with more negative feelings through school, church, or activities – loneliness, frustration, shame. Just like the secure base, this negative cycle will carry into the working world, but may lead to feelings of isolation or delayed development.

Again, our language can often be casual. Instead of confidence in social behavior, we see someone who is withdrawn and shy. We often label this type of behavior with the catch all phrase of "insecurity." While this is right on the one hand – as it is opposite of a secure base – the truth is more complicated. Insecure behaviors come in many different forms and some of these behaviors have advantages in the working world that will be highlighted in this chapter.

As you can see from the way attachment styles are formed, they generally do not change much over our lives. They may adjust a slightly with experiences, but because we enter situations with a pre-conceived mental model and add the experience to that model, it is hard to adjust the style significantly. There is research that shows a significant life event can dramatically shift our attachment styles, but these are not common.[3] The more common reality is that our attachment styles drive much of our behavior in the working world. These styles determine how we show up at the office, how we interact with our colleagues, why we form relationships, how we set our priorities, and often how we respond to change in the organization.

While research agrees that Secure is an attachment style, there is some debate related to how to categorize the other styles. Some suggest there are only two other styles – Ambivalent and Avoidant.[4] Our research demonstrates three clear other attachment styles – Dismissive, Preoccupied, and Fearful. However, we do not use these words for describing workplace attachments. The traditional words have clinical meanings that have come to carry certain judgments with them that we do not intend to imply within the workplace. Instead, we use a different approach that allows for a more rounded view of each style. We use the following language in the workplace:

- Secure = Stable
- Dismissive = Autonomous
- Preoccupied = Distracted
- Fearful = Insecure

We are going to use these workplace definitions for the remainder of the book, as they are much more palatable for discussion among colleagues – Stable, Autonomous, Distracted, and Insecure. These four styles are defined by a combination of factors on a continuous spectrum of anxiety and avoidance. Anxiety in this context is exactly the way it was described in Chapter 2. It is the level of worry and concern that an individual feels based on their instinctual reaction to life experience. Avoidance is a measure of the person's sociability with others in the organization and includes how a person feels about others around them.

As you can see in Figure 4.1, those with a Stable attachment style maintain low anxiety, while demonstrating low avoidance. Somewhat similar, but different, the Autonomous attachment style is also low on anxiety, but is not highly social. This group is sometimes seen as having higher views of themselves than others. The Distracted come to work with high anxiety. It may not be driven by work, but it shows up at work. However, when they try to engage heavily at work, it can lead to colleagues realizing, and feeling, their anxiety. The Insecure have high anxiety and high avoidance.

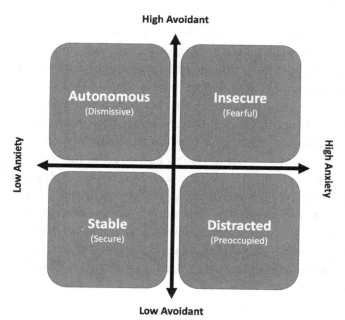

FIGURE 4.1
Attachment styles in the workplace.

They do not participate effectively in the workplace and can sometimes be seen as hiding.

Let's go a little deeper into each one:

Stable

Stable individuals generally come to work with a positive attitude and have positive interactions with others. They have a positive view of themselves and a good understanding of their self-worth. They also have a positive view of others and tend to have the ability to easily trust, build relationships, and cooperate with others. Stable individuals will often have a strong goal orientation in their work. When combined with their strong sociability, it leads to the willingness to work alone if they have to and to work in teams when collaboration is required or provides more value. They are willing to sacrifice their independence and credit in order to develop relationships with people in the organization. Stable individuals will not step on people to get ahead. This group may develop strong acquaintances at work or may not, that might be more situational. By and large, this attachment style tends to report high levels of engagement in the office and strong employee satisfaction.

Stable individuals have a strong sense of what a secure base means and they strive to get back to that level emotion. Like everyone at work, Stable individuals face times of challenge and conflict. They tend to address these periods by leveraging their secure base and using this to regulate their emotions. Again, this does not mean they lack frustration, but that they will quickly get back to balance. Therefore, if anxiety spikes, they will try to bring back to balance. If they have a negative interaction with a colleague, they will seek to repair it out of respect and value for the relationship.

The overall regulating function that comes with the Stable person makes this style less susceptible to reductions in performance level due to internal or external strife. Meanwhile, this same mechanism explains how this style can maintain both strong ambition and strong relationships. Stable individuals can gain social dominance through their attractive style and their goal-based orientation rather than through power-based or coercive techniques.

There are two challenges for the Stable attachment style. The first is a blind spot for the other attachment styles. It even comes across in the way this chapter is written. There is a subtle implication that a secure base is the right or the only way. That is not the case. However, those with a strong Stable attachment may be unaware of the other styles around them and how those styles impact their colleagues. What may seem easy for the Stable person may be a challenge for another style and the Stable person may not appreciate that difference. It is often unawareness, not arrogance that leads to this perception. Stable individuals can improve their standing with others by looking through the lens of attachment styles and trying to be aware and understanding of the three other styles. The second challenge for the Stable attachment style is related to empathy. Recent research related to attachment styles and leadership (we will discuss further in Chapter 8) indicate that the lack of fundamental awareness of the other three attachment styles combined with the blind spot mentioned above can equate to a perceived lack of empathy or an actual lack of empathy, especially during times of change.

Autonomous

Autonomous individuals often come to work with relatively low anxiety and without much, if any, desire for social interaction. This attachment style is often characterized by individuals who have difficulty building relationships with others. The Autonomous attachment style emerges for those who have learned to cope without much support or nurturing. They tend to operate on their own with high goal orientation and they tend to believe that they do not need close relationships for success. In fact, the Autonomous person often values this independence and self-reliance as part of their personality.

The Autonomous person can send the message that they are closed for business. Since they do not value relationships, they do not seek them. This type can have a high degree of distrust. They also worry about the possibility of rejection and, in turn, put up barriers (consciously or subconsciously) that will deter others from building connections. Even if the Autonomous person is working well with a colleague, the slightest hint of rejection may cause the Autonomous to break the relationship. This can become reinforcing cycle of loneliness for the Autonomous employee as the only way to accomplish work becomes through self-sufficiency. The Autonomous person often ends up working alone making it even harder to develop the important social-relational networks to create Stickiness within an organization.

The result is a perception that these Autonomous individuals have a high view of themselves and a negative view of others. These perceptions can be reinforced by the belief that the Autonomous must protect themselves. Whereas many may view an Autonomous person as aloof, they may view themselves as reflective or mission focused. It can lead to team members feeling abandoned or disrespected without the Autonomous person even appreciating that it happened. Therefore, the Autonomous person can be incredibly productive, even a high performer, but can negatively impact overall productivity of the organization through their behavior.

Despite the emphasis on the negative, the Autonomous style has positive attributes. The economy has many roles that benefit from such a task-focused mindset. While teamwork and managerial functions may be difficult for the Autonomous individuals, there are many positive roles for Autonomous individuals. Data-driven roles where judgment and problem-solving reign supreme will appeal to the Autonomous person and will not challenge their relationship-wary side. Moreover, these individuals can also seem quite calm in the face of extreme challenges, due to their dispassionate, almost distant, approach to the problem at hand. A simple way for Autonomous individuals to engage effectively with co-workers and colleagues in collaborative settings is to turn the process into one of intertwined cogs in the machinery. Imagine that without the other individuals' skills and information it would be impossible to accomplish the task. If this is true, then the Autonomous person may be able to collaborate effectively simply out of the shear necessity of the process.

Distracted

Distracted individuals are high on engagement. In fact, they are so high on engagement, that sociability and relationships become a hallmark of their work. They often have such strong relationships (or even just a single very strong single relationship) that drives their engagement in the organization. This can be an incredibly strong form of attachment to the organization because the Distracted individual has close acquaintances at work.

The Distracted attachment style can become detrimental because the Distracted individual can lean on a single close acquaintance so heavily as to become dependent on another person. The Distracted person has not only high engagement, but also high anxiety, and the Distracted person can use another as the offset for their own deep concerns. As a result, the

Distracted person can demonstrate a sense of low or minimal self-worth and constantly seek validation from one or many other people. A Distracted person may not have effective boundaries and may be very open about their anxieties with the people around them. This can be draining for a team and lead to a negative cycle of distancing from the person.

When it comes to workplace activities, the person may seem more concerned with looking right than doing right. A Distracted person can become so dependent on the affirmation of others as to lose perspective on the objectives of work. Such an extreme case may not speak up in meetings or take independent positions in discussion without seeing which way the team is going. Such individuals may not even take on tasks or responsibilities unless they believe they will receive positive feedback for the activity. Distracted individuals can struggle with productivity because they are doing what they perceive to be the right thing to please others instead of to meet the job expectations.

However, the Distracted attachment style is common and has a great deal of value. First, it is rarely extreme. Many people score low on avoidance and have a low to medium anxiety score that would place them in the Distracted box compared to a fully Stable position. This lower form of anxiety might be called "imposter syndrome" and might come with a healthy questioning of the positional authority of the person. Second, this mild form of anxiety along with high sociability can be highly attractive for teams and co-workers, as it is often the core of humble or servant leadership. Third, the Distracted person does create strong attachments with organizations and people, which can be incredibly valuable for building the culture of an organization. This commitment to people and institutions is a value that be nurtured toward positive and effective engagement in an organization with coaching around appropriate boundaries. The Distracted attachment style has great value during change. More to come in Chapter 8 related to the relationship between leaders and followers, but it is significant to note that strong attachments to the organization and/or colleagues can provide valuable temporary support for others during transition.

Insecure

The Insecure attachment style leads to high anxiety. As we discovered in Chapter 2, Insecure behavior is a negative extension of the FEAR emotional system. It becomes activated through poor attachments early in life that led to a cycle of ineffective attachments. This anxiety likely has nothing to do with work, but it becomes a dominate characteristic in the workplace where the Insecure person is unable to manage their anxiety effectively.

The style is demonstrated above on our chart as high on anxiety and low on engagement. However, in most cases, it is not that these individuals are low on engagement, but that their high anxiety causes them to struggle with engagement. The Insecure often want close relationships with both peers and managers. Insecure individuals seek others to support their own validation, but their anxiety makes it difficult to trust others and depend on others for support. Even though the Insecure may be committed to deep relationships and connection, their deep FEAR of rejection makes it hard for them to express their feelings. This creates a cycle of distance between the Insecure person and others. An Insecure person's FEAR leads to skepticism of others that is felt, which results in distance from others, and ultimately leads to some cynicism from the Insecure person.

Unlike the Autonomous their distance may not be productive, as this style's struggle with anxiety may make them much less productive. There are two possible challenges here for an Insecure person. The first is that they will ignore relationships and focus on work, but that the relationships will still be a desire and distraction. As a result, they will not be able to focus on work and will be unable to be productive. The second is that relationships will be sought and reciprocated, but that the Insecure person will "over think" the relationships due to hypersensitivity. This might lead to the same cynicism, but through exhaustion and burnout.[5]

Despite all the concerns expressed about the Insecure type, these individuals can provide value in organizations. The Insecure person's desire to Stick to people and an organization is laudable. They want to be a part of a team, so force them into team settings. It is incumbent upon leaders to leverage their contributions and their skills while mitigating some of their potential challenges. However, it may not be wise to put them on long-term projects until they build some confidence in an organization. Let them build up trust in multiple places across an organization to build attachment to the organization and not a single person or team.

This style-type needs open communication to support trust and needs opportunities to build their rapport with others. Research on effective teams suggests that each team should have a team skeptic that pushes back on the assumptions of the group. An Insecure person might effectively play that role in a smaller group, serving to push back on others for what may be the unanswered questions or confusing information in the group and using this approach to build trust with others.

ATTACHMENT STYLE INDEX© (ASI)

The Attachment Styles Index (ASI) is a unique survey tool designed around the concepts of attachment styles and the impact they have in the workplace. Unlike other tools, the ASI gets away from the relationship-based questions of other attachment style assessments and professionalizes the concepts for the workplace. The tool is comprised of 25 questions that are a combination of quantitative and qualitative questions. The ASI uses a seven-point Likert scale and can be administered in eight to 10 minutes. The quantitative questions are standard and have been statistically validated for both value and exclusivity over years of research. The qualitative questions vary based on the organizational scenario. The ASI results for the organization define a distinct perspective on both the individual and more broad organizational attachments.

The ASI yields a report on each person's attachment style and the aggregate styles of the organization. These can be viewed by department, division, or team, depending on the most appropriate breakdown for the context. Since 2018 the ASI has been use across over 16 organizations and has been administered to more than 2000 individuals in four countries.

Over the years, we consistently observed that there is no one correct attachment style. Different styles can thrive in different organizations and in different situations. In fact, as we will discuss in Chapter 8, different styles work with different leaders, too. Often the ASI is used in situations of current or future change. Leaders find the ASI valuable in identifying the characteristics of individuals that will influence others during change and those that will more readily accept or resist change based on their attachment styles.

HOW TO THINK ABOUT ATTACHMENT STYLES AT WORK

There is no one right type of attachment style. The highly Autonomous can provide value to the highly-charged work environment by bringing balance to what might be an extremely dramatic workspace. Conversely, the Distracted might provide support to those who are equally struggling with anxiety, but unable to be social enough to discuss their concerns. There is no one right type of attachment style and each provides different value in different situations. However, attachment styles have been underserved as a tool for assessing individuals in the workplace. There are five areas where attachment styles have proven predictive of other behaviors organizations try to assess:

- Personality Types
- Work Tactics
- Collaboration
- Ethics
- Behavior during Organizational Change

Attachment Styles and Personality Types

Studies have shown that attachment styles may serve as the backbone of the common personality types that many organizations already test as part of professional development programs. Many personality tests assess some version of the "Big Five" personality traits, which anchor to five factors of personality:

- **Openness to Experience** – inventive/curious vs. consistent/cautious
- **Conscientiousness** – efficient/organized vs. extravagant/careless
- **Extraversion** – outgoing/energetic vs. solitary/reserved
- **Agreeableness** – friendly/compassionate vs. critical/rational
- **Neuroticism** – sensitive/nervous vs. resilient/confident

The Big Five, like attachment styles, emerge in our youth and remain constant through most of our life. Studies that compare subjects on both ratings of Attachment Style and the Big Five demonstrate a clear association between the approaches. Perhaps unsurprisingly, Stable individuals score lower on neuroticism and higher on extraversion, while having higher levels of conscientiousness. Consistent with our descriptions above, the Insecure and Autonomous both have higher associations with neuroticism. The two styles also have a lower connection to extraversion and conscientiousness. The difference between the Insecure and Autonomous is around agreeableness, where the Autonomous are significantly less likely to demonstrate agreeableness than the Stable or Insecure. There does not appear to be a strong distinction between the different styles when it comes to openness to experience.[6]

Attachment Style and Work Tactics

In a fascinating study of over 500 undergraduate students at a large Midwestern university, Patricia Hawley et al. sought to answer the question of whether attachment styles led to how individuals would engage others in their goal attainment strategies. The group of researchers wanted to understand why some people use coercive behaviors such as aggression and power to persuade others to move toward their goals compared to those that use more social and attractive approaches of persuasion. They found there were five types of tactical thinkers:

- Low Tacticians: Low in both coercive and prosocial tactics
- Average Tacticians: Average in both coercive and prosocial tactics
- Prosocial Tacticians: Use the prosocial tactics more than their peers
- Coercive Tacticians: Use the coercive tactics more than their peers
- Dual Tacticians: Use both the coercive and prosocial tactics more than their peers[7]

The researchers found that attachment styles effectively explained the tactical choices of many participants. Coercion seems to be a sign of the Autonomous. Both the coercive and dual tacticians aligned with the Autonomous style. Their high sense of self-worth, confidence, and willingness to engage with people, but their lack of close relationships allows this type to freely move between more aggressive behavior to achieve their goals and more social behavior, when it aligns with their objectives. The risk with this group is that the social behavior may be based more in deception – gossip, information gathering – as the Autonomous will deploy the prosocial tactics only as a means of using people as a resource toward their goal attainment. They will use charm when it works and force when charm fails – think Machiavelli.

On the other hand, the prosocial tacticians leverage their relationships for equal attainment of self and others. Their profile aligns with the Stable style and they tend to think about how to engage others for "win-win" goal achievement. The Stable lack concerns of betrayal and loss of relationship, so they value the social tie as much as the goal attainment. The Stable style may also lead someone to lack a preference for tactics. Both the low and average tacticians demonstrate moderate engagement, good confidence, and low levels of anxiety in the Hawley study. This suggests that the Stable may drive prosocial tactics or may have modest ambitions that lack the need for a strong preference in tactics.

Overall, this is not surprising. The Stable will often look at achievement in terms of potential gains. As a result, they will engage with others to identify the best way to attain these gains. By comparison, those with higher levels of anxiety (be they Insecure or Distracted) will FEAR their own loss. As a result, people around them become like a resource to be leveraged. They will break any sort of social agreements (like psychological contracts) quickly out of FEAR that someone else is either: going to break the contract first or keep them from attaining their goals.[8]

Attachment Styles and Collaboration

Similarly, attachment orientations can predict whether coworkers are likely to help each other. A study of employees within an Israeli telecommunications firm, Geller & Bamberger, monitored how attachment styles predicted relationships and support among newly hired employees. The researchers profiled the new employees and their attachment styles on the Experiences in Close Relationships Scale (ECR Scale), which is more commonly used for intimacy and relationships. They then assessed the value of interactions between the participants by using a peer rating system to determine whether other employees were helpful and whether that help was significant in the employee's ability to do their job.

The study found that the Distracted and the Insecure struggled helping others, most likely due to their own challenges of anxiety and self-worth. Likewise, the Autonomous could provide help, but it was not as likely to be deemed significant or valuable. Again, the Stable style provided the strongest base for supporting others because the individuals were both low on their own anxiety and able to effectively engage with others.[9]

Attachment Styles and Ethics

As noted above, what is unique about attachment styles compared to other forms of assessment is the combination of self-perception and perspective on others in a single assessment. The combination of the two views works extremely well when looking at a topic like ethical behavior, which relies on beliefs about both self and others. In three separate studies of attachment behavior compared to ethics, the researchers Lumina Albert and Leonard Horowitz found a link between the type of attachment style and ethical behavior.

In two studies, the researchers mailed a consumer behavior survey on ethical behavior to staff at a state university in India and separately to a set of undergraduate students in the United States. The survey presented a series of statements of behaviors to participants and asked the participants to determine whether the behavior was ethical or unethical. For example; "You find an item you want that is mismarked at a cheaper price. You purchase the product for the incorrect price." In a third study, they asked managers in two different industries in India to respond to a different questionnaire about ethics in the workplace; asking them to respond to statements about rule-following in the office like "Not reporting others' violations of company rules and policies." The goal of these three studies was to work across cultural lines and organizational roles (consumers and managers) to get to more generalizable findings about attachment styles and ethics.[10]

Across all three studies Albert and Horowitz found that a person's view of others had a strong impact on how they identified ethical behavior. Both Stable and Distracted strongly affirmed that the ethical concerns questioned in the survey were in fact wrong. There was only one deviation in the findings, which came in the most severe transgressions of illicit profit, where both the Insecure and the Distracted were slightly more likely to accept the behavior. This is likely connected to the poor self-image and belief that they may not be willing to stand up for their convictions against these violations.

The most brazen acceptance of poor ethical behavior came from the Autonomous style. Across all three studies, the Autonomous group (mostly men) were more willing to accept the unethical behavior. The researcher initially thought those with a strong opinion of themselves and a poor opinion of others would be more likely to uphold ethic. However, as Albert and Horowitz note, "Apparently, a positive image of self in combination with a negative image of others leaves the person with a bold sense of entitlement, ready to transgress without embarrassment, guilt, or concern about consequences." The impact of this study is that the Autonomous may not only be hard to manage within an organization, but you may also need to watch them for unethical behavior.

Attachment Styles and Organizational Change

An organizational change is another situation when an understanding of attachment styles can be helpful. Different attachment styles respond to change in different ways. Many approaches to change management focus on moving people through the process of change with an emphasis on creating an awareness or understanding of the change to create a desire for it. However, for many people, change is about a loss, and attachment is a process that is anchored to an understanding of loss. As a result, by taking an attachment styles view, we can understand who will be open to change and who will not be open to change.[11]

Since the Stable individuals are generally resilient, change is not a huge challenge for them. Stable individuals will seek support throughout the organization and focus on problem-solving to answer the questions that arise for them.[12] As a result, they tend to feel comfortable with changes *early*, but that does not mean they are without effort. Even the Stable will need a deep rationale understanding of an organizational change before they will be comfortable with an emotional acceptance of the change. Additionally, the Stable regain their confidence quickly during a change, but often find it hard to identify how well others adapt to change. It is important for the Stable to connect with others and understand their challenges with change.

Conversely, the Distracted may try to connect for very different reasons. Both the Distracted and the Insecure will feel an underlying concern with organizational change as it will challenge their confidence and self-worth; especially in cases of significant change (downsizing, merger, role re-definition). However, the Distracted will try to connect with many people for reassurance and emotional support. This role as connectors may actually make them good leaders during change activities. That healthy "imposter syndrome" mentioned before may make them effective and empathetic listeners and communicators for others experiencing the change.

The Insecure will likely withdraw and playout their own worst scenarios without much conversation or collaboration. The Autonomous may also withdraw but may do so believing that they can "solve" the change on their own and/or it will not apply to them in the same way. Any withdrawal is an attempt to save face and protect themselves from the potential negative feelings related to the forthcoming change.

MANAGING ATTACHMENT STYLES DURING CHANGE

Over the course of the last 10 years, the central government in the United Kingdom reduced funding to local councils. Local council responsibilities include education, housing, social care for the elderly, local roads, and waste collection. In 2017, a *Financial Times* article stated that "the LGA (Local Government Authority) of local government as a whole in UK would have £15.7billion less central funding by 2020." Against this challenging financial and political landscape, local governments across the UK faced a significant change management challenge. There was now a continuous need to restructure and rationalize services based upon the available financial envelope.

One Northern England based county identified a change management framework and supporting data collection strategy as a proactive step to manage the process. The Attachment Style Index was used to define and track the organization's intent to implement and subsequently embrace change within the local council. The ASI was initially administered in September 2016 using quantitative and qualitative questions. This real-time data provided the council with a custom perspective of the change impact on their team, based on the respective attachment styles.

The data proactively informed the management team's strategy. One significant example of the data-driven strategy was the need to establish more transparent communication. The behavior shift was a transition for the organization that ultimately provided a more defined foundation to build increased trust.

During December 2017, the ASI was administered a second time to monitor a larger cohort of employees within the organization. This follow-up survey extended beyond the organizational leadership and demonstrated the positive impact of the change management strategy. Despite having a broad range of attachment styles, the county leadership was moving the organization in the right direction. The leadership team credited the success to the proactive identification of attachment styles and the effective management of styles by the county leadership.

THERE IS NO RIGHT ATTACHMENT STYLE

In his book, *The 7 Habits of Highly Effective People,* Stephen Covey outlines the process of building from a "secure base" to a state of self-mastery. Easier said than done. His lesson is to build from dependence to independence before trying to become interdependent. As we have seen, this just may not be the way we as humans are wired to interact – interdependence is part of the human brain. And some people may emerge to the working world with a solid secure base, while other may not, but they can all have value. That does not mean that individuals will struggle in their respective organizations. **There is no right attachment style.**

Each of the styles described provides different benefits for different types of roles. Table 4.1 below shows some of the characteristics that emerge as strengths for each of the attachment styles to consider as you think about how to apply these lessons in your organization.

TABLE 4.1

Attachment Style Strengths

		Stable	Autonomous	Distracted	Insecure
Personality	Openness				
	Consciousness	X			
	Extroversion	X		X	
	Agreeable			X	
	Neuroticism		X		X
Behavior	Coercive		X		
	Prosocial	X			
	Collaborative	X			
	High Ethics	X		X	
	Change Leaders	X		X	
	Detailed Work		X		X

The lesson is that the attachment styles can save organizations a lot of other kinds of research on employees. Attachment styles are cognitive, based in the intuitive functions of the brain, which means they are not likely to change or be learned over time. For this reason, attachments styles present lasting indicators of the strengths and risks of employees or potential employees who are about to go through a significant organizational change. By using attachment styles, the organization can learn how to support these employees more effectively through their work and the process of change.

PRACTICE EXERCISES

COLLECT: ATTACHMENT STYLES QUESTIONNAIRE

The considerations in Table 4.2 are NOT the Attachment Styles Index. This is not a scientific tool, but it can quickly help you try to get a sense of where you might fall on attachment style. Check off the boxes below (honestly) and see where you have the most alignment.

TABLE 4.2

Attachment Style Considerations

	Mine	Stable	Autonomous	Distracted	Insecure
I do not enjoy tackling tasks that are completely new to me.			X		X
It is difficult for me to be alone. If alone, I feel stressed, abandoned, hurt, and/or angry.		X	X		
I find myself minimizing the importance of close relationships in my life.				X	X
I often expect the worst to happen in my relationships.			X		X
I feel comfortable expressing my own needs at work.		X		X	
I feel that people are essentially good at heart.		X	X		

 APPLY: THE ATTACHMENT STYLES PLAYBOOK

Now that you have a sense of yourself, what are you going to do about it? Below is a playbook for you to work through the strengths and weaknesses of your style.

Take it to Scale: If you want to engage a team in a dialogue, think about having the team go through the questionnaire above and then mix and match the respondents based on their styles. Have each group discuss what they learned about themselves and how their strengths may help the rest of the team and what kind of support they may need from the rest of the team to support their personal weaknesses.

Stable

- Self-coach to maintain awareness of anxieties others may be experiencing
- Self-coach to listen appreciatively and respond authentically

- Create structured feedback sessions with defined actions to address feedback
- Maximize opportunities to interact with other leaders, to share your confidence and optimism.
- You may be a good candidate to lead public forums
- Structure project planning to include defined risk identification and management that you are aware of and appreciate the need to address real challenges. You will lose credibility with others if you appear unrealistically confident
- Use your growing energy and confidence to support others
- Leverage concrete success stories to promote the change
- Be conscious of the risk of operating too independently.
- Check in regularly with other leaders on their agendas and their priorities to make sure you are aligned and have not missed possible conflicts or opportunities for joint action
- Make sure to avoid setting up situations where you operate in a silo (as an individual without collaboration)
- Your self confidence and trust in others can lead you to be unaware of other challenges and other conflicting agendas

Autonomous

- Learn to observe yourself. Honestly review your own instincts, mindset, and behaviors
- Practice change of mindset – viewing others as valuable contributors to your success, the team's success, and the organization's success.
- Actively scan for positives in others
- Practice gratitude and authenticity, unsolicited positive recognition of others to reframe your relationships
- Accept personal accountability for connecting with others and building relationships. You are likely to find unrecognized skills when you practice them
- Balance cool demeanor with an appreciation for the natural anxiety others experience during stress
- Create routines to promote connection and updates from the team or peers

- Focus on positive outcomes and connections
- Awareness of impact on others is critical. You will find it helpful to thoughtfully and mindfully manage your interactions with others, and their potential impact on team success in the context of change.
- Guard against questioning the motives of others
- Your lack of engagement in team efforts may mean that the team will not feel secure with the value of your input to deliberations

Distracted

- Learn to observe yourself. Honestly review your own instincts, mindset and behaviors
- Practice change of mindset – viewing how much control others have in a balanced manner and recognizing the control you have over circumstances
- Identify your valuable contributions to your success, the team's success, and the organization's success
- Actively scan for positives in your own contributions
- Accept personal accountability for making independent decisions where appropriate
- Create routines to maintain balanced connections with peers, mangers, or others with whom you have highly dependent relationships
- Pause or reconsider when you feel inclined to connect repeatedly with others over a matter for which you have accountability
- Awareness of one's impact on others is critical. You will find it is helpful if you thoughtfully, mindfully manage your interactions with others and the impact on team success in the context of change
- Practice communicating with confidence to your subordinates. Be planful to ensure that you are delivering sufficient positive messaging about the organization's ability to handle change
- Make sure to develop healthy boundaries with others

Insecure

- Invest in positive mindsets both about self and others
- Reflect on positive experiences, learn to scan for personal successes and positive movements that reveal authentic esteem and approval by peers
- Seek opportunities to connect and build trusting relationships to build confidence
- Create open communication in all relationships
- Identify your valuable contributions to your success, the team's success, and the organization's success
- Actively scan for positives in your own contributions
- Accept personal accountability for making independent decisions where appropriate
- Create routines to maintain balanced connections with peers, mangers, or others with whom you have highly dependent relationships
- Guard against questioning the motives of others

 OBSERVE: POP CULTURE DOPPELGANGER

Often popular culture can help us solidify our understanding of concepts. Look at some of these popular television shows in Table 4.3 and see if you relate to any of these characters. Is the attachment style also relatable? Try using this grid with members of your team. Does this help demystify some of the concepts? Make it easier to talk about how styles might make us able to work with each other?

TABLE 4.3

Pop Culture Attachment Style Characters

	Stable	Distracted	Autonomous	Insecure
The Peanuts	Peppermint Patty	Lucy Van Pelt	Schroeder	Charlie Brown
The Simpsons	Marge / Lisa	Homer / Smithers	Bart / Mr. Burns	Principal Skinner / Mo
Seinfeld	Kramer	Jerry	Elaine	George
Friends	Phoebe	Ross	Joey	Chandler
Everybody Loves Raymond	Debra	Marie	Frank	Raymond
Sex and the City	Charlotte/ Samantha	Carrie	Miranda	Stanford Blatch
The Office	Jim	Michael	Stanley	Phyllis
Mad Men	Bert Cooper / Joan Harris	Pete Campbell / Peggy Olson	Don Draper / Roger Sterling	Harry Crane
Parks & Recreation	Andy Dwyer	Leslie Knope / Chris Traeger	Ron Swanson / April Ludgate / Tom Haverford	Ann Perkins
Brooklyn 99	Captain Holt	Amy	Rosa	Boyle
Gossip Girl	Dan Humphrey	Serena van der Woodsen	Chuck Bass	Blair Waldorf
Downton Abbey (Upstairs)	Tom Branson Isobel Crawley	Lady Edith	Earl Grantham Lady Mary Dowager Countess	Lady Rose
Downton Abbey (Downstairs)	Mrs. Hughes	Daisy	Mr. Carson Thomas Barrow	Mr. Molesley / Baxter
Ted Lasso	Coach Beard	Kealey / Ted Lasso	Jamie Tartt / Rebecca	Nate

NOTES

1 Thompson, P. M., Glaso, L., and Matthiesen, S. B. (2016). "Leader-Follower Dyads through the Lens of Attachment Theory. Attachment Style As a Predictor of LMX." *Academy of Management Proceedings*, 2016(1).

2 Dewitte, M., De Houwer, J., Buysse, A., and Koster, E. (2008). "Proximity Seeking in Adult Attachment: Examining the Role of Automatic Approach-Avoidance Tendencies." *British Journal of Social Psychology*, 47(4), pp. 557–573.

3 Fein, E. C., Benea, D., Idzadikhah, Z., and Tziner, A. (2020). "The Security to Lead: A Systematic Review of Leader and Follower Attachment Styles and Leader–Member Exchange." *European Journal of Work and Organizational Psychology*, *29*(1), pp. 106–125.

4 Ainsworth, M. D. (1979). "Infant-Mother Attachment." *American Psychologist*, *34*, pp. 932–937.

Boatwright, K., Lopez, F., Sauer, E., Van Der Wege, A., and Huber, D. (2010). "The Influence of Adult Attachment Styles on Workers' Preferences for Relational Leadership Behaviors." *The Psychologist-Manager Journal*, *13*, pp. 1–14.

Bretherton, I. (1992). "The Origins of Attachment Theory: John Bowlby and Mary Ainsworth." *Developmental Psychology*, *28*(5), pp. 759–775.

5 Leiter, M. P., Day, A., and Price, L. (2015). "Attachment Styles at Work: Measurement, Collegial Relationships, and Burnout." *Burnout Research*, *2*(1), pp. 25–35.

6 Shaver, P. R. and Brennan, K. A. (1992). "Attachment Styles and the "Big Five" Personality Traits: Their Connections with Each Other and with Romantic Relationship Outcomes." *Personality and Social Psychology Bulletin*, *18*(5), pp. 536–545.

Mikulincer, M., Florian, V., and Tolmacz, R. (1990). "Attachment Styles and Fear of Personal Death: A Case Study of Affect Regulation." *Journal of Personality and Social Psychology*, *58*, pp. 273–280.

7 Note, this language is different than the authors, but is more relatable.

8 Hawley, P. H., Shorey, H. S., and Alderman, P. M. (2009). "Attachment Correlates of Resource-Control Strategies: Possible Origins of Social Dominance and Interpersonal Power Differentials." *Journal of Social and Personal Relationships*, *26*(8), pp. 1097–1118.

9 Geller, D. and Bamberger, P. (2009). "Bringing Avoidance and Anxiety to the Job: Attachment Style and Instrumental Helping Behavior among Co-workers." *Human Relations*, *62*(12), pp. 1803–1827.

10 Albert, L. S. and Horowitz, L. M. (2009). "Attachment Styles and Ethical Behavior: Their Relationship and Significance in the Marketplace." *Journal of Business Ethics*, *87*(3), pp. 299–316.

11 Albert, L. S., Allen, D. G., Biggane, J. E., and Ma, Q. K. (2015). "Attachment and Responses to Employment Dissolution." *Human Resource Management Review*, *25*(1), pp. 94–106.

12 Kafetsios, K., Athanasiadou, M., and Dimou, N. (2014). "Leaders' and Subordinates' Attachment Orientations, Emotion Regulation Capabilities and Affect at Work: A Multilevel Analysis." *The Leadership Quarterly*, *25*, pp. 512–527.

Mikulincer, M. and Shaver, P. R. (2003). "The Attachment Behavioral System in Adulthood: Activation, Psychodynamics, and Interpersonal Processes." In M. P. Zanna (Ed.), *Advances in Experimental Social Psychology, Vol. 35*. New York: Elsevier Academic Press, pp. 53–152.

Mikulincer, M. and Shaver, P. R. (2005). "Attachment Theory and Research: Resurrection of the Psychodynamic Approach to Personality." *Journal of Research in Personality*, *39*, pp. 22–45.

5

What Do I Get Stuck to?

"What I am referring to…is not so much the object used as the use of the object"

D. W. Winnicott[1]

"When I was a child I depended on a bottle
Full grown I've been known to lean on a bottle"

The Avett Brothers "True Sadness"

Family-owned businesses create unique relationships with their employees. This was certainly true for Elizabeth. She was senior leader in a UK-based publishing house that was owned and operated by the same family for more than 60 years. While the company focused on developing first-rate content for readers, the leadership focused on developing first-rate people and colleagues. Elizabeth developed from a junior copy editor into an executive while with the company and she was planning to continue her career in the industry and with the thriving company.

The company was not only family-owned, but it also felt like a family. The relatively small business of 150 employees was collegial and maintained a casual work environment. The family owners were ever present in the activities and operations of the firm. The family's interests were even woven into the culture of the organization. The current president was an avid art collector, and he kept much of his collection in the office for the entire company to enjoy.

Then, three years ago, the family decided to sell the company.

Elizabeth was stunned. Everyone was stunned. But the timing was right, the market was ripe, and a much larger American publishing house was ready to take over the reins. The owners once again treated the entire company like family. They worked with the acquiring company to ensure that

DOI: 10.4324/9781003157458-5

all employees would maintain their jobs. Some people decided it was time to move on, others decided to retire, but by-and-large the company stayed intact as the organization transitioned to new ownership.

Then the president did one more thing. He offered for each employee to take an object with them – a piece of art from the art collection he had been building and collecting around them. Some of the art was incredibly valuable – Picasso, Rembrandt – and some of it were pieces the president found in West End flea markets with his keen eye for talent. With this range of value and talent on full display, he stood before it the entire time to say goodbye and thank you.

The entire team went from the most senior employee to the most junior employee to select a piece of art. Some chose the high value art and called it a retirement investment, others took a sentimental piece that hung near their desk. Elizabeth chose a small painting of lilacs by a French artist from the 19th Century that she had never heard of until she joined the company. When everyone was done, Elizabeth looked around the room to find 150 people standing with 150 paintings. Some of the paintings were small and held tightly by her colleagues. Some team members were casually leaning on the paintings. And some of her friends chose larger paintings that were leaning on them.

Elizabeth is still with the publishing house. There have been a lot of changes over the last three years. She learned the American buyers kept their word on job security, but they had a different way of doing things. More of her colleagues exited, while others worked incredibly hard to make the new merger a success. On one long night she was reading over another manuscript by an academic trying to write their first novel. It was a tough read. She looked up from her desk and saw the lilac painting. She smiled. It was good to know some things never change.

For Elizabeth and the publishing house, artwork was a powerful object that helped people through a difficult transition in the organization. They were likely about to lose many things they liked about their company as it merged with bigger and foreign company, but the artwork served as a last reminder of their former family-owned employer. Moreover, by giving the employees the ability to choose the piece of art, the owner was not telling each employee how to feel about this transition, he was simply offering them an outlet for their emotions and creating a shared experience of the process of selecting art together.

We know that objects are an important part of how people get Stuck. Remember, we **lean on tangible and/or intangible objects for support**. The process of using objects throughout our life is a little like going across a set of monkey bars. Early in life we detach from our earliest caretaker and grab that first bar for a new attachment then as we outgrow it or it becomes unnecessary we move to the next bar. We move from object-to-object to create new support throughout our life. We know that people form attachments in the Intuitive Brain, which is a combination of memories, emotions, and learning. Objects play an important role in the process because they serve as memories, activate emotions, and can support learning. In this way effective objects can help create Stickiness and support someone who is Stuck.

In the chapter we will explore:

- How do we Stick to different objects in our lives?
- What are the different types of objects that we Stick to?
- How can objects support us when we are Stuck?
- What are the different objects that can help us transition to a new future?

WHAT WE STICK TO

As we have discussed, attachment behavior begins at birth and carries into adulthood. It is the human need to lean on tangible and intangible objects for support. Therefore, it stands to reason that the form of those objects would change as we grow. Just like the story of human evolution itself, attachment objects shift from one's caretaker to an attachment to other people, places, and things in our daily life. Early humans were dependent on following the land's production to determine where they lived and for food and nourishment. However, as they gained the ability to grow their own food, they became more capable of building a base-location and then moving into other locations to explore opportunities in other geographies. Likewise, as we move beyond our initial attachments, we find an ability to express our attachment behavior in different ways.

Attachment behavior starts with an individual, but quickly evolves to groups and organizations. Think of your own developmental experience.

Did you ever find yourself trying to explore how you "fit in" during your teenage years? Did you ever wonder where your group might be? You might have been looking for the next social-emotional connection that would serve your attachment behavior. As John Bowlby notes,

> During adolescence and adult life attachment behavior is commonly directed to groups and organizations ... other than the family. A school, a college, a work group, a religious group, or a political group can come to constitute ... an attachment figure ... and is a straightforward continuation of [a more sophisticated] form of attachment behavior.[2]

And remember, attachments are not just to people. In the earliest days of life, children often comfort themselves with physical objects to take the place of the missing caretaker. These objects may come to symbolize a relationship, but the attachment is now to the object and not an individual. The same can be true with intangible concepts like ideas that drive behavior, whether it is the loftiest concepts of democracy and freedom, or principles of religion, or something close to home like a motto or saying. These attachments are equally valuable in serving for attachment behavior.

We commonly see four types of objects that represent the tangible and intangible objects our team members lean on at work – relational, organizational, cultural, and locational. Each type has both tangible and intangible elements, and most people have some attachments within each of these groups. Rarely do people lean on just one of these types of objects. Let's go through each of them.

Relational Objects

Attachment behavior starts with the caretaker, so it makes sense that attachment to other people is one of the possible attachments that occurs in the workplace. Over time, our attachment behavior evolves from connection to a single individual in a caretaker capacity to different types of relationships. The core of this concept goes back to our brain development as social beings that seek to collaborate and minimize risk by sharing the workload with other. One of the most common relational objects is the relationship between co-workers. These are strong bonds that can form the core of whether employees decide to Stick with an organization.

In over thirty years of research, Gallup Research has advocated the importance of a single question in employee engagement in the workplace – "Do you have a best friend at work?"[3] The question gets at the heart of relational attachment in the workplace. Gallup consistently finds that people who have a best friend at work are more engaged in their company. More importantly, the research demonstrates that by creating even more personal relationships at work, companies can improve workplace safety, customer satisfaction, and bottom-line profits. The strong relationship that we saw for Jenna in the opening story is one that bodes well for Jenna's connection to the company over the years.

Another type of relational attachment is that of the leaders. Of course, there are different kinds of leaders. There are those leaders who exist in a managerial capacity to provide directive support and guidance, and there are those leaders who exist more in an aspirational, but distant capacity. The more directive leadership or supervisors can create a certain type of relationship within the workplace, which is an important attachment in the workplace. Gallup's research is instructive here, too. In their eighty-year review of the Gallup workforce data, Jim Clifton and Jim Harter describe the attachment in their book *It's the Manager.* Clifton and Harter note that managers can be the key to successful Stickiness within organizations these days, finding that 70 percent of the variance in employee engagement is tied to the manager with merely 15 percent of today's workforce feeling engaged at work.[4]

That's right. Only 15 percent of today's workforce feels engaged at work and most of the variance for employees is tied to their manager. This makes sense. The successful manager builds a bridge between the theoretical notions of the large-scale company and the real work of each team member. The correct behavior is a natural extension of effective attachment behavior, as Crowell and Treboux note, "attachment figures in adult life need not be protective figures, but rather they can be seen as fostering the attached individual's own capacity for mastering challenge."[5]

Beyond the direct supervisors, there are leaders in both the workplace and beyond the workplace that impact the workplace as attachment figures. Leaders in large bureaucratic organizations can loom larger than life. Employees can often refer to them by their first name, as if they are in the hallway, even in large organizations. Figures like Jack Welch at GE, Steve Jobs at Apple, or even Katherine Graham at *The Washington Post* had this persona whereby the employee base often discussed working *for* these individuals even though the three may have never been their direct supervisors.

In these cases, the attachment to the leader is so strong that it sounds like the connection that some have had with leading political leaders. For example, the oft-told story of the collapsing man at FDR's funeral train who was approached by a neighbor who mistakenly believed the man had a personal connection with the former president. The neighbor asked the grieving man, "Did you know the president?" And he responded, No, but he knew me."

And it can even extend beyond the organizational leader. Imagine working all day long at Dairy Queen as a young aspiring business tycoon. While you are spinning delicious Dilly Bars, you are really thinking about your leader and wondering how you can learn from him to continue to grow your personal wealth. Your attachment might be to Berkshire Hathaway Chairman Warren Buffet that fully owns the ice cream chain and many other businesses. This kind off attachment to leadership is strong and has an impact on how employees show up and stay at work.

Organizational Objects

The organizational realm represents the attachments that individuals make with organizations. We form different types of attachments with organizations. These can be the relational attachments that are mentioned above, but sometimes they go beyond the relational aspects. Organizational attachments might be to the products of the organization or perhaps the physical structures of the organization (like the office). Conversely, organizational attachments might be even less tangible, such as the mission, vision, philosophy, or values of the organization. Perhaps even just organizational processes might represent the attachments for some to the organization.

When it comes to product connection, commercial advertising is often helpful in illustrating the attachment that employees might have to products. Brand loyalty is certainly a form of attachment and it is easy to see how one's own preference for a product might lead to excitement to work for/ with a particular organization. In 2010, Proctor and Gamble began overtly leveraging this connection with a set of advertisements around the many "Thank yous" that are owed to mothers. It began with the 2010 Olympics and featured professionally made ads that showed how moms helped athletes do all the little things to help them from the start of their journey to the peak of their career. The idea was that P&G products were there alongside moms for the journey and therefore, P&G was the other thing you, as the consumer, should be thanking. The campaign, called "Thank you Mom" has driven millions in sales for P&G and builds the connection between the customer and P&G products. There is no doubt that this kind of loyalty, demonstrated in the ad campaign, that exists between customer and product can exist between employee and product, too.

ORGANIZATIONAL ATTACHMENT OBJECT: THE PSYCHOLOGICAL CONTRACT

The psychological contract is a perfect example of an organizational attachment. Do you remember your early school days when you first started talking about government? Perhaps you had a teacher that introduced an experiment like this: *Work with three to four of your fellow students. Imagine you can define a new country with a new government. What would the government look like?*

In this discussion, young minds describe how they would they never punish anyone or never make anyone go to bed before they want. Eventually, they will start to normalize around what they need to form a cohesive society – rules, law, governance. For many young people in the western world, this is how we are introduced to the idea of the social contract. It is a powerful mental model that underscores much of western society, whereby mutually agreed upon concepts and ideas lead to laws, administration, and ultimately enforcement that compels behavior.

In the organizational world, we have a parallel construct, known as the *psychological contract*. It is a particular mental model focused on a relationship between one individual and either one other individual or an entire organization (either one-to-one relationship or one-to-many). Like the social contract, it is the unwritten set of rules and expectations that exist between an organization and employee. Just like in the governmental example above, there is a formal and enforceable legal contract for employment. This document codifies the work expectations and the payment gained for services. However, the psychological contract covers beliefs, behaviors, and perceptions within the organization.

The notable business theorist Chris Argyris first mentioned the term in 1960 and John Kotter conducted his doctoral research on the topic of psychological contracts. Denise Rousseau studied the concept deeply and advanced research around core elements of the psychological contract including respect, compassion, objectivity, and trust. In recent years, the topic has made an interesting resurgence via Amy Edmondson's work on the role of psychological safety in the workplace, as safety becomes an underpinning of the contract.[6]

The core of the psychological contract is that there is some reciprocal understanding between the organization and the individual that goes beyond money. Given that payment for services can be done at many organizations, the psychological contract serves as the core answer to *why* people do many of the things they do in organizations – put in more hours than they are paid for, recruit their friends to the organization, or advertise their organization via clothing or car decals. The psychological contract is the mechanism for the *Stickiness* that a person feels to their organization. When it is working, they feel supported, trusted, and valued. However, an organizational breach of the psychological contract can be damning for an employee who may lose trust and decide the organization is no longer worthy of their work, their support, or their effort.

Additionally, employees can build attachments with the purpose of the organization, even if the product is less tangible. What underlies P&G's campaign is that their product might be packaged, but their purpose is a feeling that runs deeper than packaging. This purpose drives many employees. As Simon Sinek most notably attests in his book *Start with Why*, purpose drives value for products, movements, and organizations. Leaders who start with why will drive employees to create more value for the company and themselves.[7] The reason is that purpose is a form of attachment that helps bring someone closer to the organization. Whether is stated as a mission statement or a vision, these simple statements help form the bond for an employee that their job means more than just producing dollars for Wall St. For many employees, this attachment is what will drive them to do more and create a greater sense of loyalty in the organization.

Sometimes, the attachment at the organizational level is not about the product or the overall purpose of the organization, but about the *way* the organization conducts business. For some, the process of work matters greatly, and a streamlined or efficient process might be a reason for someone to appreciate one workplace over another. Alternatively, a particular type of process might drive Stickiness for an employee. For example, technology developers may prefer either a Waterfall approach or an Agile approach; project managers may have their preferred set of tools; and process improvement experts might even have their own preferred processes. In all these cases, the approach to work itself might be the driver for keeping someone connected to a particular organization, because the employee likes their comfort with how work is done in the organization.

Locational Objects

The locational area represents the attachments we make to the geographic places in our lives. These may be represented by neighborhoods, communities, towns, counties, or countries. The key is that it is a connection to physical location that is made unique by the people and the culture of the location. Sometimes, the distinction can seem somewhat inseparable, as the land creates cultural tendencies that are unique for the location. However, the attachment itself is to the land, not the other potential realms. A simple analogy comes from wine tasting and the French concept of *terroir* – that the grape is shaped uniquely by the soil. In this same way, the attachment of the individual is uniquely affixed to the land.

At a community level, one can imagine the stories of individuals that have suffered through natural disasters or troubling economic situations but refuse to move on from the location because "it is all they know." At the geopolitical level, this concept plays out in the concept of citizenship. There are some countries in the world for which a connection to the land is sufficient to claim citizenship. The concept called *jus soli* applies to more than 30 countries around the world, including most of the Americas and, most notably, the U.S., Mexico, and Canada. This concept known as birthright citizenship has driven global migration patterns as many people strive to come to North America for the birth of child to receive citizenship. *Jus soli* is purely connected to the land as the sole measure of someone's right to be a citizen, compared to most countries of the world that follow a combination of *jus soli* and hereditary-based concepts of *jus sanguinis* (or "of the blood").

In the workplace, locational attachments can emerge at the organizational level or within the organization. At the organizational level, think of the many manufacturing companies that highlight their connection to the United States with the "Made in America" emblem on the logo. One such company, WeatherTech, has made it a significant part of their value proposition to customers by noting in nearly every advertisement "Proudly Made in America." Of course, they are appealing to something greater than just a locational attachment, but that is certainly part of the story.

The more common effect of locational attachments in the workplace comes within an organization, especially a multi-locational organization. As organizations grow, either organically or through acquisition, they often develop locations in different regions of a metropolitan area, state or province, country, or even across multi-national lines. Leaders should expect that as this happens, certain locational attachments will emerge from these different offices. These locational attachments may first appear to be local pride and can be a positive thing that create comradery in a given office.

However, these locational attachments can also have two negative side effects. First, they can be used as a wedge between the location and other locations (including a headquarters). Local leaders and teams can start resisting organizational leadership with stories of "how things are done around here" that can be a challenge to manage. Second, locational attachments can be a precursor to a siloed organization. Locational attachments can have the impact of limiting an individual's willingness to explore and create relations with "others." This limitation in a global company can lead to suspicion and concern about people from other locations, even within the same company.

Cultural Objects

Cultural attachments can be the most nebulous and the most challenging to address, however, they can be the most important to understand. Cultural attachments can exist at an organizational level or they can transcend organizations into societal levels. Like organizational attachments, cultural attachments often come in the form of intangible objects that have some sort of physical representation. These symbols or artifacts represent a deeper idea such as a religious belief or a political philosophy that has become represented by a physical symbol. Many such global artifacts from religions (icons, statues, jewelry) and governments (flags, badges, memorials) embody the concept of cultural artifacts. These cultural objects create deep emotional connections to feelings in us as individuals.

The notable cognitive linguist George Lakoff has spent a lifetime looking at the connection between language and our attachments. Lakoff's work reveals how our brain uses "conceptual metaphors" to contextualize not just a sentence, but an entire situation and even our cultural context.[8] A common example of a situational concept might be a debate, which Lakoff may describe as an extended metaphor of a verbal argument or (in other words) war through language.[9] In turn, the common phrases of the language all connect via war-like structures – win, loss, defense, strategy, outflank, shoot down, counter. Another might be the electoral process, which is conceived of as a "race." The candidates run, they are winning, they are ahead, behind, trailing, etc. However, it is a singular vote at a point in time, there is no actual race.

These metaphorical constructs impact not only the language the participants use, but also behavior of the participants. In fact, it might even shift the incentive structures for the individuals. Our debates become more contentious because the winners in war matter, therefore, the winners in debate must also matter if we are using the language of war. Likewise, the race that is run for electoral success becomes elongated and (in western democracies for sure) starts to influence policy before the next race has started. The behavioral shift that ensues is an unending electoral season, constant campaigning, and non-stop fundraising, because the "race" is never finished.

Perhaps Lakoff's biggest contribution to cultural objects are the linguistic metaphors around *Moral Politics*.[10] Thinking about the metaphors above, Lakoff describes two dominant metaphors that explain the differences in political beliefs between liberals and conservatives in the United States. In a clear attachment construct, Lakoff describes how both sides view the value of governance through a deep mental model (or metaphor) of the family. Conservatives, he offers, view government more like a dominant father who must create rules, systems, and enforcement for the children (the citizens). Liberals, on the other hands, use what Lakoff calls a "nurturant parent model" that assumes a balance of parental guidance (mother and father) protecting children from the negative influences of the world.

Lakoff's metaphorical paradigm is represented the language and imagery that each political side uses in their speeches, their campaigns, ads, and fundraising. Lakoff argues that these tactics intentionally evoke a connection to the emotions represented by this core and fundamental metaphor, which is perhaps, one of the strongest and most foundational cultural attachment objects in American society today. The oft-discussed divisive political culture, self-sorted media conglomerates, and duopoly of political ideas[11] rests upon this core cultural attachment.

In the context of the workplace, the culture is the *esprit de corps* established by the organization. As we will discuss in Chapter 6, attachment concepts become a powerful tool for examining and building a Sticky culture within an organization. However, an organization rarely maintains complete control over its culture. Each employee comes to the organization as a member of other societal groups through which they will bring their own cultural understandings and attachments. Within an organization these other cultural elements (along with locational elements) blend with the culture the organization attempts to establish to create the true organizational culture.

Cultural objects have their positives and their negatives. As we have seen in the United States in the early 21st Century, many statues and artifacts of the past bring two meanings to people. Cultural objects of attachment often take this characteristic, as so many items are left to interpretation. The challenge for the workplace is to balance these cultural objects in a way that allows those who need these objects for support to use them without isolating others. In most cases, the law has stepped in to help organizations manage these challenges around religious and political objects, but there are always some items that enter the workplace that fall into a new area for exploration.

THE ROLE OF OBJECTS WHEN WE GET STUCK

As we discussed in Chapter 3, objects play an important role in the attachment process. They help soothe young children and help them separate effectively from that initial caregiver. There is always a time when the child must separate from this caregiver. This period can create some anxiety and the child can often find an object to lean on to help them through it. This separation has some important characteristics:

1. It is the first time a young child views the caretaker as separate from themself
2. It creates a state of confusion for the young child
3. It is a process for the young child to separate from the caretaker[12]

Likewise, adults have evolved this same logic into an understanding of the transition process. It is no longer about connection to a caregiver, but rather the relationship of the adult to the reality of the world around them. Does the world around them look the way they expected? We often label this process in the organizational world as Current State and Future State. However, when we define the situation in binary terms of Current and Future, we miss the important lesson characteristic number 3 above – there is a process. The process for the young child has three phases to it: 1) Current State 2) _____ and 3) Future State.

There are many names for this second phase. Kurt Lewin developed his model for how people go through change in 1947. He also described three simple phases. He used the concept of ice for his model with the "Unfreezing" as the first phase, the "Change" as the second phase, and the "Refreezing" as the third phase.[13]

From a clinical perspective, this is called the "Transitional Space." The Transitional Space can activate four important elements of the emotional systems we highlighted in Chapter 2:

1. FEAR can be activated via the anxiety and confusion at the uncertainty ahead, even for adults;
2. SEEKING can be activated, which can lead to creativity, helping people find art, religion, and scientific breakthroughs;
3. PLAY can be activated which serves to both engage and sooth someone;
4. CARE can be activated as a person feels the support of another person.[14]

As a result of these factors, as Lewin noted, the Transitional Space is a place where change can happen.

The Transitional Space is a place of both concern and opportunity. It is an area between two extremes, so the Intuitive Brain (the Limbic System) releases old memories coupled with old emotions and recouples those emotional systems with new memories. But, these same memories can just as equally be coupled with negative emotional systems that lead to continued anxiety and resistance.

The difference between these two can be whether there is a support mechanism for the person while they are in the Transitional Space. The support system can come from an object that helps the person productively engage with the emotions in the Transitional Space; something that yields creativity, PLAY, and CARE instead of anxiety. Additionally, this object can help engage in the other components of the Intuitive Brain (memory and learning) to support overall behavior change.

Transitional Objects

These kinds of objects are called transitional objects. They are a specific type of object designed to help someone move from their Current State through the Transitional Space to a Future State. Since we know that people get Stuck in their Intuitive Brain, we know we need to help them become Unstuck in the same place. The Intuitive Brain includes memory, emotion, and learning. In the section above, we talked about how emotions can be hindered during the Transitional Space. Furthermore, we know that when emotions are challenged, and someone feels loss (from Chapter 3) they may shut down or retreat from engagement. This can make it difficult for us to guide them through the Transitional Space to the other side where they will find a Future State.

This is where we employ a transitional object. An effective transitional object helps someone with the feelings of loss and either supports the anxiety that could potentially turn negative or counteracts that potential anxiety by positively engaging the other emotions around creativity, PLAY, or CARE. For creativity, the transitional object could be something as simple as a pad to draw on and allow the mind to wonder. For PLAY, it could be a simple game that helps the team member learn about the new change. For CARE, it might be another team member taking an interest in a struggling team member as an effective support mechanism.

We know from our study of the brain that the emotional side is only one third of the battle. What is powerful for an effective transitional object is that it can provide the emotional support **and** support learning at the same time. An effective transitional object can help support the individual in the behavior that needs to change. For example, if an individual needs to remember to enter their work time on a regular basis, a transitional object might be a simple and entertaining sticker that goes in a strategic place in their home or office to remind them to enter their time. If a team is anxious about losing a trusted leader, a transitional object might some sort of stress "toy" that helps them to relieve their stress while thinking about that loss rather than bringing in a new person that might take some time to become a trusted support mechanism.

Over the years, we have seen a few different types of transitional objects used in different organizations with varying degrees of success. There are a few final characteristics that create strong transitional objects to help people get Unstuck. First, they should provide the right kind of emotional support to a person. Second, they should support someone's learning when the change requires a new behavior. Third, there should be a lasting connection to the cultural values of the organization. Fourth, there should be some connection to the change that the person might be going through (e.g., the transition from the Current State to the Future State). Fifth, when possible, there should be some sort of personal value in the object. This last one is always the hardest to quantify because we never quite know what will resonate with each person, but the goal is to connect with many people. The easiest way to think about it might be to think about the connection to different attachment styles.

In Table 5.1, the objects can provide different levels of support through a transition to different types of people. It is probably obvious, but in a large organization no one object will work for the entire enterprise. A mix of objects will be necessary to get the entire organization to move from a Current state to a Future state.

For many, the strategic alignment of a change to the overall sustainment of the organization (the mission) would be enough. However, others need a connection to a path forward, even if all the answers are not yet known. For these individuals, the change process itself with its detailed plan of what is to come ahead becomes the transitional object. Still others find comfort in a feeling of what the future may hold with either the comfort, excitement or even a vision of what is to come. These folks may say, "I need to see it to make it real." For this group the sensory experience matters and it is a critical transitional object to help them through the Transitional Space.

Gamification is a special version of sensory experience, as it has immense power to both provide a version of the future that employees can see and control, while simultaneously training them in new behavior. When this

TABLE 5.1

Transitional Objects

Object Types	Examples	Emotional Benefit	Learning Benefit	Org Value	Change Value	Personal Value
Mission	Mission Statement Strategic Plan Purpose Statement Core Values	SEEKING	Not Likely	Yes	Yes	Secure Preoccupied
Process / Approach	Agile DMAIC LaMarsh PMP Prosci	SEEKING FEAR	Possible	Maybe	Maybe	Secure Dismissive
Sensory Experience	Office Scent Music or Song Video Visuals	SEEKING FEAR CARE PLAY	Possible/ Likely	Maybe	Maybe	Secure Dismissive Preoccupied Anxious
Gamification	Wearable device data Apps – games Wargaming sessions Video games	SEEKING FEAR CARE PLAY	Highly Likely	Yes	Yes	Secure Dismissive Preoccupied
People	Charismatic Executives New Leaders Designated Representatives Change Agents Town Hall Sessions	SEEKING FEAR CARE	Highly Likely	Yes	Yes	Secure Preoccupied
Physical Symbols	Offices Awards Cultural Artifacts Displays *Chachkies*	SEEKING FEAR PLAY	Possible/ Likely	Yes	Yes	Dismissive Preoccupied Anxious

type of sensory experience is combined with the competitive spirit of games, gamified learning takes on a new role in the transitional space. It has a unique power to hit the Intuitive Brain with memory formation, emotional elements, and learning at the same time. It also provides a positive reinforcement via "bragging rights" and sometimes even physical rewards that can make gamification a powerful tool in change management.

Still others can be guided by trusted leaders who serve as the transitional objects for safe passage from the Current State to the future. We will say much more about the unique role of both formal and informal leaders in Chapter 8, but the role of transitional object is one that every person in an organization can play. Lastly, some appreciate physical objects for support during transitions. Large organizations often invest in branding materials during large-scale transformations. Sometimes these giveaways or *chachkies* are trendy or cheap, but there is missed opportunity for intentionality. With a representative giveaway that supports the behavior sought via the transformation, the organization can reinforce new behavior.

TRANSITIONAL OBJECTS: STONES THAT FLOAT VALUES

In 1914, Edwin Booz started what would become the first management consulting company in the world called the Business Research Service. The company would evolve into Booz Allen Hamilton, which is now over a century old and has more than 27,000 employees around the world. At the company's centennial, the modern leadership wanted to redesign the corporate values to create a strong foundation for the second century. Through a series of dedicated workshops involving more than 150 participants across all levels of the company and outreach interviews to every location, team, and role in the firm, the company established a new purpose statement – *Empower People to Change the World*.

The statement was accompanied by five values and accompanying statements to clarify how team members would demonstrate each of the values. As corporate values go, Booz Allen's value are unique for their boldness:

- *Unflinching Courage*
- *Passionate Service*
- *Champion's Heart*
- *Collective Ingenuity*
- *Ferocious Integrity*

The previous values had been around for decades. They were 10 single words that were the kinds of language that had become generic in corporate cultures. The leadership team for the transformation needed a roll-out strategy as bold as the new values. The new values were etched into a set of polished stones and given to the Senior Partners of the firm. However, they were not to keep the stones. They were to give away the stones to the members of their leadership team that demonstrated the values. The leaders held meetings with their team, talked about the values, what each meant to them, and then gave a stone to a person who demonstrated the value. In this way, each level of the organization rolled out the new values, not through instruction, but by demonstration.

The process created three transitional objects at the same time. Imagine you are a middle manager in the company hearing the presentation from your trusted leader. You hear your leader describing the value in detail – Transitional Object 1, "my leader is telling me to behave like that." Then your leader takes a physical object (a nice one at that and gives it to your colleague) – Transitional Object 2, "I want that." And now you have a peer who is seen as the personification of the abstract concept of a value – Transitional Object 3, "I want to be like them." The process creates triple reinforcement for the behavior.

And did it work? Six months after the roll-out, 83 percent of employees said they could explain Booz Allen's purpose to someone else. In the annual leadership survey that occurred eight months after the roll out, "living our purpose and values out loud" was ranked as the top component that leaders felt empowered to drive. Over time, the values were supported with other tools like cards and lanyards that went to all employees, but even three years after the roll-out many employees keep the one, two, three, or, in rare cases, all five stones they collected on their desk. As one employee put it, "stones help keep these alive."

As you read this chapter, it might be deceptive to think, "I can just control people with objects." You cannot. First, remember that adults use all kinds of objects for support and team members in your organization likely have healthy and effective attachments established within your organization to objects that you may need to change one day. So, it is important to remember that – today's favorite object may become tomorrow's object of change. As you try to leverage transitional objects, be wary of dependency on any objects in organizations, as this dependence can lead to an unhealthy attachment for anyone.

Second, a transitional object alone will not help you get someone Unstuck. The object must go together with many things (to be discussed in Chapter 8), but most importantly, a supportive environment. For the transitional object to support someone in the Transitional Space, the person must first be brought into the Transitional Space in a supporting way. This takes an effective awareness of what is happening and why, as well as an effective appreciation of the person's position within organization. In short, the organization must show mutual respect for the employee before asking the employee to buy-in to the transitional process. This kind of respect comes from a strong relationship between an employee and a leader, which is where we are going next on our journey.

PRACTICE EXERCISES

 ### REFLECT: FIRST TRANSITIONAL OBJECT

Do you remember an early transitional object? What was it? Was it a person? An item? A stuffed animal? A blanket? Did you hear stories about your first transitional object? Was it a pacifier? A stuffed animal? Or another person? When you think back on your early youth, do you tend to remember certain people, places, things? It can be helpful to understand how we first transitioned to and from situations to think about how we may transition in the workplace.

 ### OBSERVE: ATTACHMENT OBJECTS INVENTORY

In this chapter, we explored four types of attachment objects: Relational (R), Organizational (O), Locational (L), and Cultural (C). It's time to take stock of some of your attachment objects. As you go through a typical day at work, what are the items that make you feel comforted? What helps you feel like you have control when things get difficult? When you get bad news or a difficult email, what do you turn to?

TABLE 5.2

Attachment Objects Inventory

Situation	Object	R	O	L	C

Make a little chart like Table 5.2 above and track yourself. You will be identifying how the attachment objects support you through your attachment response. Where do you lean? More relational? More locational? More cultural? What do you think this tells you about yourself?

When you think about your peers in the organization, what do you think their chart looks like? What objects do they lean on for support?

 APPLY: CREATE A TRANSITIONAL SPACE

The most effective way to break an attachment to an object is to bring someone into a Transitional Space where they can experiment with the idea of letting go of the object. The Transitional Space is when the Current State and the Future State are both known, but the Future State is not yet accepted. One of the characteristics of the Transitional Space is a propensity for playfulness and creativity. As a result, sensory experiences and creative experiences can be quite helpful in creating a Transitional Space.

By sensory experiences, we mean those things that require senses that are the normal thinking part of your brain:

- Listening; music, podcasts, TEDTalks
- Smelling; flowers, gardens, herbs, cooking, essential oils
- Tasting; coffee, tea, food
- Seeing; art, TV, visuals
- Physical; walking, exercise, meditation, a shower, a fan in your face

By creative experience, we mean:

- Cooking
- Painting
- Building
- Cleaning/organizing (for some, no judgment)
- Decorating
- Singing

The point in all of these is to actively think about the change you are facing as you start the exercise and let the activity take you away from your thought process to see if the activity calms you. As it does, it should release you to think about the change in a different way. You have entered the Transitional Space and the activity has become the creative outlet to allow the emotions to regulate and let the other aspects of your brain think out how the change impacts you.

Take it to Scale: You can take this activity to scale by having a group work through the process of doing a creative task to demonstrate their feelings about a change effort. It can be simple like collaging via magazine photos about the change, but the act will help get past the attachment reactions into the Transitional Space.

NOTES

1 Winnicott, D. W. (1971). *Playing and Reality.* New York: Routledge, Introduction.
2 Bowlby, J. (1969). *Attachment and Loss, vol 1: Attachment.* New York: Basic Books, pp. 207–209).
3 Mann, A. (2018). "Why We Need Best Friends at Work." *Gallup.* January 15, 2018. www.gallup.com/workplace/236213/why-need-best-friends-work.aspx.
4 Clifton, J. and Harter, J. (2019). *It's the Manager.* New York: Gallup Press.
5 Crowell, J. and Treboux, D. (1995). "A Review of Adult Attachment Measures: Implications for Theory and Research." *Social Development, 4,* p. 297.
6 Argyris, C. (1960). *Understanding Organizational Behavior.* Homewood, Il: Dorsey Press.
   Edmonson, A. (1999). "Psychological Safety and Learning Behavior in Work Teams." *Administrative Science Quarterly, 44*(2), pp. 350–383.
   Kotter, J. (1973). "The Psychological Contract: Managing the Joining-up Process." *California Management Review, 15*(3), pp. 91–99.

Rousseau, D. M. (1989). "Psychological and Implied Contracts in Organizations." *Employee Responsibilities and Rights Journal, 2*(2), pp. 121–139. https://doi.org/10.1007/bf01384942

Rousseau, D. M., and McLean Parks, J. (1993). "The Contracts of Individuals and Organizations." *Research in Organizational Behavior, 15*, pp. 1–43.

7   Sinek, S. (2009). *Start with Why: How Great Leaders Inspire Everyone to Take Action.* New York: Portfolio / Penguin.

8   Pinker, S. (2006). "Block That Metaphor!" *The New Republic.* October 9, 2006.

9   Johnson, M. and Lakoff, G. (2003). *Metaphors We Live By.* Chicago: University of Chicago Press.

10 Lakoff, G. (2016). *Moral Politics: How Liberals and Conservatives Think, Third Edition.* Chicago: University of Chicago Press.

11 Gehl, K. and Porter, M. (2020). *The Politics Industry: How Political Innovation Can Break Partisan Gridlock and Save Our Democracy.* Cambridge: Harvard Business Review Press.

12 Grady, J., Grady, V., McCreesh, P., and Noakes, I. (2020). *Workplace Attachments: Managing Beneath the Surface.* New York: Routledge, pp. 114–115.

13 Lewin, K. (1947). *Field Theory in Social Science.* New York: Harper & Row.

14 Szollosy, M. (1998). "Winnicott's Transitional Spaces: Using Psychoanalytic Theory to Redress the Crises of Postmodern Culture." MLA Convention, San Francisco, CA.

6

How Does Culture Get Stuck?

"Perhaps the most intriguing aspect of culture as a concept is that it points us to phenomena that are below the surface, that are powerful in their impact but invisible and to a considerable degree unconscious. In that sense, culture is to a group what personality or character is to an individual."

Edgar Schien[1]

"We believe that it's really important to come up with core values that you can commit to. And by commit, we mean that you're willing to hire and fire based on them. If you're willing to do that, then you're well on your way to building a company culture that is in line with the brand you want to build."

Tony Hsieh

Right before the pandemic shutdown, Patrick started working with a new client in the financial services space. He went into the office to learn more about the company and the new engagement. He was supporting a digital transformation, but anytime he goes into a new office he finds himself investigating the culture.

Patrick was given a point of contact prior to arriving that was the client's chief of staff; he gave the name to the front desk security guard in the lobby who led him to the elevator. When he got off the elevator onto the mostly glass floor of the 50th floor, Patrick was instantly struck by the view of Manhattan. He was met by a receptionist, this time employed by the company, who was sitting at a solid steel and glass desk surrounded by the view – the desk was empty aside from a phone and a keyboard. The receptionist was dressed casually in jeans and a T-shirt. He thought, "Shoot, I am overdressed again." She took his coat and escorted him to a conference room.

Along the way, Patrick noticed a few interesting displays. First, a timeline of the company's financial success, from formation to present with some

DOI: 10.4324/9781003157458-6

of the major milestones along the way. Second, another timeline demonstrating the company's contributions to a set of charitable organizations along with pictures of the team members actively volunteering for different groups. There were also some impressive pieces of art that were almost too large for the narrow hallways but were still striking. And there is one more thing he noticed; all the senior executives had offices on the interior of the building, while many of the team members sat in open cubicles out in the sundrenched open space.

The conference room had an equally impressive view and the receptionist offered him a cup of coffee. Patrick asked if he could get it myself (he never missed an opportunity to make his own coffee as it helps him see where he will get the next cup). The snack room was as nice as the conference room. A range of fresh fruits, dried fruits, nuts, teas, and coffee. A nitro-cold brew coffee, sparkling, and still water. The provisions for a modern working coffee break.

Patrick went back to the conference room to be greeted by the CEO and his CTO who were both in jeans and casual shirts. He really did overdress. The CEO greeted Patrick by saying, "So, what do you think of our wall of fame?"

Patrick was confused. The CEO excitedly took him to a different hallway where there was an entire set of pictures that were grand works of art, but homemade drawings by children.

The CEO said, "Each month one of our offices volunteers with Ronald McDonald House and the challenge is for the office to send in the best drawing from a child along with the 'favorite' as voted by the kids. As you can see, the kids have a sense of humor."

Many of the pictures were labeled with names like, Kenny age 7 and Jessica age 10, then others said Thomas age 25, Frank age 32, Bob age 62. "Is this one yours? It's terrible." Patrick sheepishly said to the CEO.

"Isn't that great?" he said with a boisterous laugh.

As we walked back to the conference room to discuss digital transformation, Patrick asked him his burning question, "Why the office? It doesn't seem to fit with your culture."

Again, the laugh, and the CEO said with a smile, "Sometimes, in this business, your client wants a show, but you need to make sure your team knows who we really are."

As the story above demonstrates, there is something unique about this financial institution. They have all the trappings of a fine New York financial house, but all the casual nature and humility of a local barber shop. That's what makes the organization unique, and it provides a differentiated position in the marketplace. For those who want exclusivity, you've got it with the security, the top floor, the view, and (as we came to learn) well-dressed financiers. For those who want a company with a casual work-life balance, the company seemed to offer that, too. **But**, for their team members, this was one culture that was characterized by the phrase "protecting wealth for families." This was their culture. We work for families – our client's and our own.

If you are trying to get something to Stick or Unstick, it will not happen without an understanding of culture. And yet, the formation of culture is an attachment process and creating organizational culture is about creating Stickiness for your organization. Therefore, working through, instead of against, attachment will be the way to create, affect, and change culture.

In this chapter we will explore:

- What is culture and how does it relate to getting Stuck?
- How can we create a culture that Sticks?
- What is the challenge when our culture gets Stuck?
- How does culture overcome difficult situations?

WHAT IS CULTURE?

In a 2017 survey of 1,348 of executives from across North American public and privately owned corporations nearly 92 percent agreed that improvement in "corporate culture would increase your firm's value." At the same time, 65 percent agreed culture was very important at their company and more than half of the executives agreed that culture was a "Top 3" part of their value proposition as a firm. With all this emphasis on the value of culture in a firm, only 16 percent of the executives agreed their culture is "where it should be," meaning they need to work to optimize their culture.[2]

It's clear that culture has a value. It makes one wonder – how many executives really know the culture of their organization? It is not meant as an individual challenge to any one executive more a question of how hard it is to understand culture. Culture is difficult to define in any organization and even harder to manage. So, what is culture?

Culture is the way *we* do things here.

In any group or organization, culture represents the guidebook, the rules of the road, for that organization – what is acceptable, what is not acceptable, what will be lauded, what will be laughed at, what will be rewarded, and what will be punished. It is unique to the group, at whatever level you choose to explore, and often it is hard for any one person to describe it within the group. Often it takes an outsider to identify the culture in an organization. That is because organizational culture comes with a few complex paradoxes of culture that relate to the elements of attachment we have discussed in previous chapters:

- Culture is both seen and unseen
- Culture develops social cohesion and supports market value
- Culture is both intentionally created and unintentionally co-created
- Culture often has an internal meaning and external meaning
- Culture is both singular and siloed

Seen/Unseen

Organizational culture has two parts to it – the seen and the unseen. The visible side of culture is the symbols, the stories, the mythology, the artifacts, the acronyms, the jargon, the offices, and even the people that we observe when we walk around an office or interact with an organization. In short, it is all the objects that are unique to that organization.[3] The unseen side of culture is the deep set of shared assumptions, beliefs, and values that bring these objects to the organization. The American organizational psychologist Edgar Schien calls culture an iceberg, explaining that we see a small part of the culture when we look around, but it is beneath the surface where we will find why these objects represent the culture.

As we discussed in Chapter 5, objects can often serve as attachment representations for other concepts. In the case of culture this can have a double meaning. The physical object can be the source of the individual's attachment and at the same time the object may also be a representation of the deeper belief system of the organization.[4] As one set of researchers called it, organizational symbolism or "those aspects of an organization that its members use to reveal or make comprehendible the unconscious feelings, images, and values that are inherent in that organization."[5] For example, in our opening story the casual attire of the office might be highly valued by the team members because it represents a difference between the company and their competitors. And as William G. Dyer, the organizational culture and change researcher, notes, "it is the perspectives, values, and assumptions that are central because they embody the interpretation of the artifacts, thus representing the belief system behind the artifacts."[6]

Social Cohesion/Market Value

The cultural elements of an organization play an integral role in creating market value and integrating people into the organization. Market value is created by the efficiency and effectiveness that is gained by having consistent, predictable, reliable products, solutions, and service to customers and clients. This can be attained without having social cohesion, but organizations that have a higher reliance on people will inherently have a higher reliance on a social base to deliver these results. Therefore, a strong cultural base is necessary for new members of the organization to learn the routines and procedures that yield maximum market value. For many organizations, this economic incentive, and the ability to adapt with market conditions drive the desire for cultural cohesion.[7]

As individuals learn the rules of the road, they understand what it means to succeed and fail in the organization. These rules also establish norms around what is acceptable behavior in the organization and what is just and right. Collectively, these cultural norms set a common language for the organization to share beyond the "standard operating procedures" of work. This creates a feeling of group membership and ultimately a more effective and committed workforce, which also makes the group more resilient to change.[8] As we discussed in the Chapter 2, Stickiness resides in the Intuitive Brain where memory, emotion, and learning are co-located. It is important for new team members to feel the emotional side of the culture (like the objects and deeper values) while learning the organizational structures, guidelines, and procedures to make these more routine elements feel like more than just activities.

The most effective way for this socialization to happen is through the process of social mimicry through which a new team member internalizes the importance of not only the work, but the behaviors that represent the culture.[9] There is a wonderful scene in the movie *Office Space*, where the character played by Jennifer Aniston, Joanna, is being asked to put on more pieces of "flair" as part of the culture of the restaurant Chotchkie's, where she works as a server. She doesn't want to. Her manager asks her to look at her co-worker Brian who has on 37 pieces of flair and she says, "So you … you want me to wear more?" The manger must take a side-step to explain the purpose of the flair and what it means to the culture. While we are not supposed to be on the manager's side, it is a good example of how social mimicry can work. If Joanna was more interested in the job, she might be more willing to follow Brian's lead.

Intentional/Co-Created

Likewise, culture is produced in two different ways – intentionally and unintentionally. Intentional culture is developed by organizational leadership creating the conditions of culture – mission statements, strategy, objectives, values, and objects that support and align to this vision. In an effectively aligned organization, employees will see and feel that this alignment exists through intentional behavior from the top down. This might take the form of physical objects like organizational charts, systems, processes, routines, manuals, and performance programs. **But**, the unintentional culture emerges in two different ways: 1) the implementation of these physical objects and 2) the history or mythology behind these objects.[10]

CIVIL RIGHTS AND MUSIC: CO-CREATING TRANSITIONAL SPACE AND A TRANSITIONAL OBJECT

The U.S. Civil Rights movement is far from over. Social change that was sparked four centuries ago became a righteous flame in 1960s America only to find its embers return recently in the wake of more violence against Black Americans. However, it was in the protests of 2020 that something became apparent as a missing element from the landscape compared to its historical predecessor. The Freedom Song.

In the 1960s, protests were often coupled with a soundtrack of protest songs that came straight out of the hymnals of the local church. Many members of the protest movements grew up hearing one of the tunes or verses in their local pews as a child. As the movement evolved, freshly minted songs emerged in the same spirit, but they came directly out of the gospel tradition. Songs like "We Shall Overcome," "Keep Your Eyes on the Prize," and "Go Tell It on the

Mountain" were not only a way to create a common cause, but they also created protection and a mental escape. As Rutha Mae Harris noted, the songs were the same "Only thing we had to change was a lyric."[11]

Jamila Jones is one of the founders of the Harambee Singers and an attendee of the famed Highlander Folk Center where she participated in writing a verse of "We Shall Overcome." Jones tells of one night while at the Highlander Folk Center when the police came in to break up the group in darkness. The police had billy clubs and guns, while the young people sat in darkness with nothing. Someone began singing quietly the words, "We are not afraid." Jones goes on to explain:

And we got louder and louder with singing that verse, until one of the policemen came and he said to me, "If you have to sing," and he was actually shaking, "do you have to sing so loud?" And I could not believe it. Here these people had all the guns, the billy clubs, the power, we thought [pause] and he was asking me, with a shake, if I would not sing so loud. And it was that time that I really understood the power of our move – of our music, how powerful it was that this – it unnerved him so much that he had to come and ask that I not sing so loud.

And I can just tell you that I got louder and louder. And somehow even the nature out there in that darkness, because everywhere was dark, but it looked like our voices blended that night to the point of complete harmony and beauty. And from then on, I knew exactly how powerful our songs were.[12]

What happened with the Freedom Songs of the 1960s is that they were at once familiar enough to create an attachment, emotional enough to move the singers into a transitional space, and shared in a way that created a shared experience. That new memory connected with emotion and older memories was now a new attachment. And when it yielded power over guns it could be used in times of strife.

As Rutha Mae Harris explains, these songs were an attachment to a youthful experience that helped many protestors to at once unite and escape back to an emotionally safe place even when facing difficult times. Harris notes "Without those songs, I don't believe there would have been a movement" because "It took away a lot of fear." Harris recalls the uncertainty of every protest. They may end in threats, prison, or violence (if only from the other side). In an interview, she recalls a police officer with a drawn gun: "We never knew what to expect; we didn't know whether we would get shot or whether we would get beat up. That's when the songs came into play, they kept me from being afraid."[13]

Music is linked to emotion. It can open a transitional space where both a common past memory can be shared, and a new memory can be created simultaneously. This powerful emotional experience creates a different kind of experience that opens a transitional space, a new attachment, and, over time, a unique culture for the Civil Rights movement. There are certainly protest songs today. They represent some powerful and emotional music. But they are created for mass consumption of the message to change hearts, not mass unity to galvanize minds.

First, the implementation process of culture is often where unintentional culture starts. Ironically, the unseen elements of culture have the greatest impact on how unintentional culture develops. It is not how the values are written by the leadership, but how they are lived by each member of the team *and* how they are reinforced by the leadership through even the most casual of settings. Think back to our opening story. The leadership took two casual intentional steps to try to encourage part of their desired culture – they put a visual of financial performance for the entire company (shared success) and terrible drawings by their team members from all over the country (individual humility). If this behavior is followed by promotions of people who only look out for themselves, it will not work. The culture will break, but if the team around the country rewards the people who are demonstrating performance and teamwork, that will set a different tone.

Second, there will be cultural elements cocreated with the members of the organization. These are sometimes referred to as latent cultural elements.[14] These are the dormant beliefs and assumptions that team members bring to the organization when they join and that mix with others in the organization along with the organizational goals to create new elements of organizational culture. While this may feel like losing control of the culture for more controlling organizations, it is a promising sign for an organization. As we discussed in Chapter 5, when individuals are creating elements of shared memories with the organization, they are in a transitional space, which means they are willing to share not just a Current State, but also a Future State with an organization. In short, they are committed.

Internal Meaning/External Meaning

Culture tells a story within an organization and outside the organization. For the financial firm at the start of our chapter, they intentionally wanted to adjust that story based on the audience. Most organizations want to tell the same story both internal and external to the organization. However, the issue above of cultural co-creation gets much harder as we move beyond the walls of our own organization. Mythology can be created and spread. The objects come with emotions and start to represent more than just the shared assumptions and beliefs of the organization. They represent the shared beliefs of others, too. Or worse, there can be two different realities experienced around a culture.

Look at Figure 6.1. It is a law enforcement badge. It is one symbol that takes people in different directions. For the officer, it is a representation of the authority that has been granted to them as an officer of the law. For many civilians, it is a sign of safety in their community and stability. In the

FIGURE 6.1
Police Badge.

United States and around the world, some see the image and no longer feel the safety intended. What sits under each of these views is a deep set of assumptions and beliefs that leads them to each perspective about the culture represented by a single object. What does this object make you think? What would people say about the objects produced by your organization?

Singular/Siloed

Within an organization there is likely to be one dominant culture, which is a culture that expresses the core of the organization. But that may not be the only culture in the organization. There may be many subcultures or mini cultures that exist across the departments, divisions, or geographical entities within the organization. Often, regional offices create their own unique traditions or activities that yield some subtle differences in culture for that region. This can feel like co-creation, with a central culture losing control, but it might be the way that some people or localities are attaching to that culture.

Subcultures are not inherently a problem. In fact, in larger organizations, they may be a necessity to sustain effective connection through the organization as it grows. They can be a way for people to create local or shared memories around the parent culture that allows the culture to sync into the mind for the individual or group. In this way, subcultures can be beneficial. The key is that these subcultures need to unify back to the overarching culture.

THE OPPORTUNITY TO MAKE CULTURE STICK

Attachment principles underly all these concepts of culture and effectively support individuals in an organization. The core mechanism at play is the supporting function that cultural elements and objects provide individuals as they transition into a new organization. Now the question becomes – how do we build the right culture to create Stickiness in an organization? First, we know that new team members come to an organization with two feelings: 1) motivation to succeed and 2) a desire to fit in. Second, we also know that individuals need to learn about the new organization they are joining. Last, we know individuals are coming to the organization with some need to create an attachment with a support object that will help them through this transition.

In short, new employees come to the organization in a transitional space ready to soak up a culture. So, let's throw some objects at them and it should Stick ... Wrong!

There is the individual attachment to attachment objects is not the same as attachment to the culture. It's complex. There are three factors at play:

Factor 1: Individual attachments to objects

Factor 2: Collective agreement of cultural attribution of the objects

Factor 3: Individual agreement that the object is a representation of organizational culture[15]

We know from Chapter 5 that an individual forms attachment to all kinds of objects. Let's imagine a new employee named Katherine comes to our organization. She may form attachments to objects to create a sense of safety in the organization or due to her attachment style. We know that uncertainty creates stress for almost everyone. As people join new organizations – schools, teams, volunteer opportunities, work – they seek the familiar face because familiarity creates a sense of comfort.[16] Therefore, Katherine may form an attachment with Jane (who is just like her) out of simple comfort. Or it may be a result of her attachment style. Perhaps Katherine is a preoccupied person seeking someone as a support object in her new role. Either way, this connection is her choice. That's Factor 1.

Factor 2 is the collective agreement that her choice in object is part of the culture of the organization. Sticking with our example above, if Katherine selects Jane as an attachment object, we need to know if Jane is a good example of the culture of the company. Katherine is likely to mimic Jane. If Jane is a perfect example of the culture of the company, then over time this will become clear to Katherine. Other people will affirm Jane's alignment with the company's culture and talk about how Jane "fits in." However, perhaps Jane is not a "fit" and should move on from the organization. This could lead to Katherine having an adverse reaction toward the company.

This is where Factor 3 comes in. Does Katherine think of Jane as part of the company culture herself? Does Katherine think Jane is an integral part of the company experience? Do the two of them have a connection that is independent of the company *or* is it solely dependent on their time at the company? Moreover, is it so valuable to Katherine that without Jane the company loses some value for Katherine? If their friendship transcends work, then Katherine may need to find another attachment on the job, but she may be willing to Stick with the company. In fact, she may be the one who fits in!

Of course, the process is rarely as conscious as described here. It is often much less conscious.[17] And mimicry is not the only way to make culture Stick. As mentioned above, there is intentional work that organizations can do to "nudge" culture along.[18] This is done through clearly defined incentive structures that measure cultural behaviors at the same level of importance as outcome-based performance. There are limitations to this approach, as there are often unintended consequences of driving measurement of cultural elements, which can often be difficult to quantify and even more difficult to support with evidence.

Some employees may resist overt attempts to make them align to a culture. However, studies have shown that by-and-large employees who disagree with a culture do tend to attrit.[19] The more challenging situation is when leaders believe they are driving one sort of culture and the employees (usually via middle management) are casually driving another version of culture. This where an unfortunate reality of our previous section sets in – culture is an interdependent act between leaders and the led.

Swedish management scholar Mats Alvesson says it best, there is:

> …a lot of the interest in, and hope attached to, the idea of organizational culture as a vital element in management control. It is related to the attraction of (a) the possibility of moving the entire organization in a similar direction and (b) to do so through idealistic means (ideas, values). This has led to great efforts in managing specific, often strongly visible and explicit forms of symbolism.[20]

However, there is only so much that can be accomplished. Culture cannot be engineered, but merely understood, respected, and enhanced with greater levels of trust between the leaders and the led. We know that when there is alignment between leaders, the led, and the situation, that there can be great culture.

Take the story of Google. You must look past all the perks and incentives you may have heard about the Google culture to see it. Laszlo Bock is the former vice president of people operations at Google. He describes

Google's work environment in detail in his book *Work Rules.* But what Bock says at the very outset is that he hopes people can learn from Google's culture without trying to replicate it. Outsiders often look at Google and see an amazing culture of stuff. They see great facility design, collaborative workspaces, assets on campus (like a dry cleaner, a bank, rental cars), free food, and innovative technology experiments that employees support. That's the tip of the iceberg ... that's what's visible.

But what it takes to understand that visible culture is the underlying philosophy and assumptions that align to create these spaces. The underlying assumption and governing philosophy are even more remarkable. And it is summed up in one quote from Bock:

> All it takes is a belief that people are fundamentally good – and enough courage to treat your people like owners instead of machines. Machines do their jobs; owners do whatever is needed to make their companies and teams successful.

Google has no problem providing assets to its employees because it does not think of them as employees, but as owners, as partners, in building the organization.

Each organization must find its own culture. What works for Google will not work for every company. That's an important lesson in building culture. The organization must look deep in its iceberg and not just copy the objects off somewhere else. And once the assumptions and beliefs that make up culture are understood; they must be developed, supported, and nurtured to help both people and organization.

The Challenge When Culture Sticks

In a heated scene from the AMC hit workplace drama *Mad Men* the lead character, and eternally struggling modernist, Don Draper finds himself up against a young woman who is asking for something more from her work. Peggy, Don's sometimes muse and sometimes nemesis, wants a sense of appreciation for the hard work she has put into a singular effort. She wants a "thank you." Don retorts simply, "That's what the money is for!"

The benefit of attachment in the workplace is that is helps build culture in a company by developing deep connections among individuals to help them feel a part of something bigger. Employees let go of objects they lean on from other parts of their life to lean on objects in the organization for support. These new attachments become the reason that they Stick to the company. The Maslowian pyramid is certainly at play in this model. Of course money comes first. People work to pay for their life. But, beyond that they find other reasons to work for one company over another company. As we have discussed throughout this chapter, culture is one of those reasons.

So, what happens when you need to change the culture that made them Stick?

When we create Sticky culture, there is always the risk it will break. It is like breaking any attachment. There will be a sense of loss. A culture change might be a slightly worse sense of loss because it might feel like breaking the entire psychological contract for the organization. Remember, there is only so much intentionality in the creation of culture, so a stated culture change is the organization stating that it will also be changing things created by the employees. Therefore, any organization needs to fully understand its own culture before it starts breaking any parts of an existing culture. Moreover, we need to assess and help adjust culture in a way that appreciates the connection between attachment and culture.

Victoria and Rachel Whitman have developed an exceptional model for assessing the Attachment Based Culture using four dimensions:

Visibility – The obvious presence of the culture to its members and how the behaviors unique to the organization will be recognized and potentially imitated.

Connection – The trust and confidence of the members with an emphasis on interdependence to highlight relational attachment within the culture.

Unity – The prominence of a singular organizational culture to unite various subcultures and promote cultural harmony instead of cultural silos.

Commitment – Dedication or commitment of the members to the organization, its mission/vision, and its core values and beliefs to measure overall engagement.

Each of these dimensions can be assessed with a series of questions to employees about the organization. This is a starting place for how to work with the culture that exists before moving to shift the organization. Leaders and change makers will be better armed to help move people through the process of culture change by understanding the current culture and attachments through these four dimensions. The outcome is a sense of the risk and an awareness of what attachments may be broken, what trust may be strained, and, perhaps, where the culture can be strengthened along the journey to help more people Stick.

PRACTICE EXERCISES

COLLECT AND ANALYZE: INVESTIGATE YOUR ORGANIZATIONAL CULTURE

Your organization's culture is a case you need to solve. Any good detective will tell you that to solve a case you will need: 1) a timeline of events and 2) hard evidence. This exercise is designed to help you crack your organization's culture by building out the timeline of culture formation within your company – both intentional and unintentional – with the subject you know best – you. From here, you can decide whether these findings can be generalized to the rest of the organization.

To do this, you will need to visualize times that you had interactions with your organization's culture. You may need to close your eyes to do this (note: we do not recommend closing your eyes while reading this book). Each piece of evidence can be put into a little timeline with Table 6.1. In order to get started:

- Think back to your interactions with your organization over time:
  - Interviewing
  - Onboarding
  - First day
  - Town Halls
  - Regular Communications
  - Quarterly Events
  - Annual Events
  - Casual interactions – the natural settings of the office
- What is emphasized in these interactions?
  - What objects?

- ○ What people?
- ○ What visuals?
- ○ What rewards?
- ○ What concepts?
- ○ What ideas?
- What does this evidence reveal about the culture of the organization?
  - ○ Is the organization more performance-focused or more people-focused?
  - ○ Is the organization more efficiency-focused or effectiveness-focused?
  - ○ Is the organization more focused on team members or customers?
  - ○ Is the organization more focused on internal needs or external stakeholders?
  - ○ Is the organization more focused on stability and control or flexibility?
- How does this evidence support the culture of the organization?
  - ○ Does it create *visibility* for the culture?
  - ○ Does it create *connection* across people and dependence with each other?
  - ○ Does it create *unity* across the enterprise or the sub-cultures?
  - ○ Does it yield *commitment* to the overall organization?

When you are done, can you look at this list and pinpoint when you got Stuck or Unstuck to the organization? What about the culture caused you to feel your commitment or cost you the commitment?

 APPLY: TESTING CULTURE CHANGE

The only way to understand whether culture can change in an organization is to conduct small tests of culture change. These small tests will teach you both the resiliency of the culture and the ability to conduct culture change. To do this effectively, you need to understand the deep underlying assumptions that support the visible elements of culture. In short, you need to document the assumptions and beliefs before you can test them.

Step 1: Document the Assumptions, Beliefs, and Demonstrated Behaviors

- Review the previous exercise. In particular, the "What Does It Reveal" column?
- What are the common themes? Do any of these themes get to a set of deeper assumptions or beliefs from the organization?
- Do these assumptions or beliefs align with the stated beliefs of the organization?
  - If so, how?
  - If not, why not?
- Group the assumptions and beliefs into four or five overarching statements. If you have fewer, that's fine, but you should not have more.
- Taking these four or five statements, document:
  - How do you see these demonstrated daily?
  - Where is a visible place that these are demonstrated?

A demonstrated behavior does not need to be a big thing. One business leader said of their organization, "Everyone holds the door for each other, that's how we show we are in this together." Another example might be around the way that certain shared spaces or common areas are used or maintained.

Step 2: Test the Waters

Once you have clearly identified a demonstrated behavior that supports the culture of the organization, you will have to be bold and buck the trend. You may need to do the opposite or at least something different to see if the culture can be changed. Develop a small modification to the demonstrated behavior that is noticeable enough to test reactions. In the example above of holding the door, you may not want to be "that person," but there may be a positive version.

For example, when working with one organization Patrick was continually irked that people would leave the coffee area so dirty. It was cleaned nightly, but throughout the day it was a mess. As if people had no time to simply wipe up after their spills. Despite all the language about values the demonstrated behavior was "We are too good to clean up after ourselves." He started cleaning it twice a day to see if others would join in the efforts. What is your version of this?

TABLE 6.1

Culture Investigation Report

Date	Type of Interaction?	What Was Emphasized?	What Does It Reveal?	Dimensions of Culture			
				Visibility	Connection	Unity	Commitment
10/2015	Interview	Values	People-focused Focused on effectiveness Focused on flexibility	X		X	

NOTES

1   Schein, E. H. (2004). *Organizational Culture and Leadership* (3rd ed.). San Francisco, CA: Jossey-Bass, p. 8.

2   Graham, J. R.., Harvey, C. R., Popadak, J., and Rajgopal, S. (2017). "Corporate Culture: Evidence from the Field." *National Bureau Economic Research*. Working Paper 23255. Accessed Electronically at: www.nber.org/system/files/working_papers/w23255/w23255.pdf.

3   Schein, E. H. (2015). *Organizational Culture and Leadership* (5th ed). San Francisco, CA: Jossey Bass Incorporated.

      Grady, J. D., Grady, V. M., Broida, A., and Wendus, J. (2016). Organizational Culture & Attachment Behavior: Consideration of the Role of Organizational Objects in Employee Attachment Behaviors. Unpublished Manuscript.

4   Rafaeli, A., and Pratt, M. (2012). Introduction Artifacts and Organization: More than the Tip of the Iceberg. In A. Rafaeli and M. Pratt (Eds.), *Artifacts and Organizations: Beyond Mere Symbolism*. New York: Psychology Press, pp. 1–8.

5   Dandridge, T. C., Mitroff, I., and Joyce, W. F. (1980). "Organizational Symbolism: A Topic to Expand Organizational Analysis." *The Academy of Management Review, 5*(1), p. 77.

6   Dyer, W. G. (1983). *Organizational Culture: Analysis and Change.* Cambridge, MA: Sloan School of Management, MIT, Working Paper #1279–82. Accessed electronically at: https://apps.dtic.mil/sti/pdfs/ADA134881.pdf, p. 2.

7   Svyantek, D. J. (1997). "Order Out of Chaos: Non-linear Systems and Organizational Change." *Current Topics in Management, 2*, pp. 167–188. Svyantek, D. J., and DeShon, R. P. (1993). "Organizational Attractors: A Chaos Theory Explanation of Why Cultural Change Efforts Often Fail." *Public Administration Quarterly, 17*(3), pp. 339–355.

8   Namenwirth, J. Z., and Weber, R. P. (2016). *Dynamics of Culture.* New York: Routledge.

      Scrima, F., Rioux, L., and Lorito, L. (2014). "Three-factor Structure of Adult Attachment in the Workplace: Comparison of British, French, and Italian Samples." *Psychological Reports, 115*(2), pp. 627–642. doi:10.2466/49.PR0.115c25z2

9   Bandura, A. (1989). "Social Cognitive Theory." *Annals of Child Development, 6*, pp. 1–60.

      Grusec, J. E. (1992). "Social Learning Theory and Developmental Psychology: The Legacies of Robert Sears and Albert Bandura." *Developmental Psychology, 28*(5), pp. 776–786.

10 Johnson, G. (1992). "Managing Strategic Change: Strategy, Culture and Action." *Long Range Planning, 25*(1), pp. 28–36.

11 Mohdin, A. (2020). " 'They Couldn't Arrest Us All': Civil Rights Veteran Rutha Mae Harris on MLK, Protest and Prison." *The Guardian*. September 10, 2020. Accessed electronically at: www.theguardian.com/society/2020/sep/10/they-couldnt-arrest-us-all-freedom-singer-rutha-mae-harris-on-protest-prison-and-civil-rights.

12 Gates, H. L. (2021). "Episode 2." *The Black Church: This is Our Story, This is Our Song.* PBS. February 16, 2021.

13 Mohdin, A. (2020). " 'They Couldn't Arrest Us All': Civil Rights Veteran Rutha Mae Harris on MLK, Protest and Prison." *The Guardian*. September 10, 2020. Accessed

electronically at: www.theguardian.com/society/2020/sep/10/they-couldnt-arrest-us-all-freedom-singer-rutha-mae-harris-on-protest-prison-and-civil-rights.

14 Alvesson, M. (2002). *Understanding Organizational Culture*. London: Sage. Becker, H. S., Geer, B., Hughes, E. C., and Strauss, A. L. (1961). *Boys in White: Student Culture in Medical School*. New Brunswick, NJ: Transaction Publishers.

15 Grady, J., Grady, V., McCreesh, P., and Noakes, I. (2020). *Workplace Attachment: Managing Beneath the Surface*. New York: Routledge Taylor & Francis.

16 Greco, V., and Roger, D. (2003). "Uncertainty, Stress, and Health." *Personality and Individual Differences, 34*(6), pp. 1057–1068.

Peters, A., McEwen, B. S., and Friston, K. (2017). "Uncertainty and Stress: Why It Causes Diseases and How It is Mastered by the Brain." *Progress in Neurobiology, 156*, pp. 164–188.

17 Lee, A. Y. (2001). "The Mere Exposure Effect: An Uncertainty Reduction Explanation Revisited." *Personality and Social Psychology Bulletin, 27*(10), pp.1255–1266.

Zajonc, R. B. (1968). "Attitudinal Effects of Mere Exposure." *Journal of Personality and Social Psychology, 9*(2), p. 1.

18 Thaler, R. H., and Sunstein, C. R. (2009). *Nudge: Improving Decisions About Health, Wealth, and Happiness*. New York: Penguin.

19 Schnieder, B. (1987). "The People Make the Place." *Personnel Psychology, 40*(3), pp. 437–453.

20 Alvesson, M. (2002). *Understanding Organizational Culture*. London: Sage, pp. 145–146.

7

Is My Organization Stuck?

"The greatest danger in times of turbulence is not the turbulence; it is to act with yesterday's logic."

Peter Drucker

"If you want to truly understand something, try to change it."

Kurt Lewin

Our health care systems have certainly proven their ability to adapt over the last few years. However, in the fall of 2017, Peter was the program manager for a digital transformation at a large healthcare system in Virginia and he was stressed out. The effort was failing. Workers across the healthcare system were extremely committed to the organization and the well-being of all the patients in their care, but nearly every part of the organization was resisting the transformation.

"We are like a cruise ship, we know our mission, but the response time is very slow." one team member said. Worse, another team member was worried that the commitment to the mission might be hurt by the poor deployment of technology. She worried key connections might be broken by the transformation, "Silos are developing and eroding the ability of employees to maintain the organizational mission."

Peter leveraged the Change Diagnostic Index (discussed more later) and discovered the organization was quite ready to adopt the change, but the leadership was mishandling the rollout. Despite commitment to the organization, the team was losing confidence in the leadership due to the pace of the change rollout. The change management that was supposed to help deploy the technology was making things worse. There appeared to be no strategy. The team asked for outside help to come in and support

DOI: 10.4324/9781003157458-7

the technology deployment because they did not feel the leadership could handle it.

Peter knew that the incredible commitment to the mission was a great starting place and that he could help people lean on that, but what else? He needed to find new approaches to change management that would support the transformation. They needed to work smarter not harder, but instead they were spinning their wheels. This healthcare organization was Stuck.

Peter faced a common challenge. He saw an organization in the middle of a transformation, but the people were struggling. In fact, they looked tired. He felt like the entire organization was Stuck. Here is the organizational challenge. Like all of us, our organizations have a singular focus – survival. Whereas the survival of the individual depends on the evolution of one person, the survival of the organization depends on the evolution of every person in the organization.

Despite our increased reliance on technology as a society, we still depend on people to run most services in our organizations. This means that the pace of change in any organization only moves as fast as the slowest person, team, unit, or division can adopt the latest change. So, when our transformation is not working, we are really saying, our organization is Stuck. When our organization is Stuck, we are really saying our people are Stuck.

In this chapter we will explore:

- What is different about an organization getting Stuck?
- What are the symptoms we can look for when organization gets Stuck?
- How can we measure those symptoms?
- What objects support people through change?
- What does this look like across a range of organizations?

Organizations are a collection of people. Therefore, if an organization is Stuck, it is simply because its people are Stuck. Let's reiterate how this happens. Each of us leans on tangible and intangible objects for support throughout their life. This is grounded in our Intuitive Brain where memory, emotion, and learning come together in a powerful way to form attachments. When we lose objects, it creates a sense of loss that causes us to get Stuck. At the individual level, the feelings of being Stuck reveal themselves through symptoms of attachment that we discussed in

Chapter 3 – frustration, apprehension, rejection of environment, withdrawal, refusal to participate, and delayed development.

At the organizational level, the collective participants come to the organization leaning on different objects for support, but we start to develop a shared understanding of support from new objects within the organization. Then, when one of those objects is removed, the organization gets Stuck. However, the organization has no Intuitive Brain where it creates a shared memory, emotion, or learning. Instead, the process is happening in each person throughout the organization. This is what makes organizational change both so interesting and so challenging, because when an organization gets Stuck, we can't look at one brain, we need to look at all the brains.

At the organizational level we can look for the symptoms too, but we have to look across people to find the organizational symptoms. These symptoms are quantifiable measures of what's going on in aggregate across the organization. Through these symptoms, we can determine not only if some people are Stuck, but whether there are organizational *tendencies* to be Stuck. These tendencies emerge through the organization's underlying interactions, engagement, and productivity. As you can see in Table 7.1, organizational symptoms are directly linked to the individual symptoms we reviewed in Chapter 3.

Of course, not everyone thinks of it as being Stuck. There are many different names for this concept. When we think of it negatively, some call it resistance. When we think of it positively, some call it organizational willingness or readiness. In the context of an organizational change, some will use the term change readiness. In any label, the underlying concept is the same. The people within the organization are either succeeding or struggling with their attachment behavior. Collectively, the group is either secure or demonstrating the need for additional support.

The aggregate impact to the organization, is an organization that demonstrates positive traits for organizational effectiveness or negative traits of organizational effectiveness. If they are positive, the employees are more likely to have effective attachments, which will lead to an overall workforce that is productive and maintains high Morale, high Motivation, low Conflict, low Absenteeism, and low Turnover. The inverse is also true. If the organization has a large employee base that is struggling with attachment behavior, the symptoms are more likely to reveal themselves

TABLE 7.1

Organizational Symptoms of Attachment[1]

Symptoms in the Individual ➡	Organizational Equivalents
Frustration	Loss of Productivity
Apprehension (Anxiety)	Morale
Rejection of the Environment	Conflict
Withdrawal	Turnover
Refusal to Participate	Absenteeism
Delayed Development	Motivation

leading to lower Productivity, Morale, and Motivation with higher Conflict, Absenteeism, and Turnover.

Our research demonstrates that these symptoms exist across all organizations at some level. The best time to understand these symptoms comes right before introducing an organizational change. Every organizational change will test these symptoms, as it will likely create a loss for some people in the organization. Whether it is a new strategy, a new leader, a new technology, or new process; someone in the organizational will have to give something up. Understanding the organizational symptoms before this happens is similar to understanding someone's attachment style – there is nothing right or wrong, through understanding comes the ability to support.

THE CHANGE DIAGNOSTIC INDEX©

In 2011, Victoria Grady and James Grady created the Change Diagnostic Index (CDI) as a way to measure these symptoms across organizations. Similar to the Attachment Styles Index we highlighted in Chapter 4, the tool is a survey with a series of statements wherein participants rate their agreement on a 1–5 scale (1=strongly disagree, 5=strongly agree). Unlike the Attachment Styles Index, the CDI is focused on elements of the organization rather than personal questions (e.g., "My organization tends to support people through their work challenges"). The survey started as a long questionnaire of over 50 questions, but over the years, Victoria has refined the survey and the questions to a critical set of 17 questions.

Between 2011 and 2020, the tool was administered over 120 times in more than 90 organizations, surveying more than 18,000 individuals. The tool has been used in private companies, public sector agencies, and in nonprofit organizations. Often the tool is used in times of change. In these cases, the tool works best when administered at three separate times – before a major change, during a change, and after a change. In this manner, leaders are able to effectively plan for a change, monitor progress against the change effort, and then determine success at the end of the change. This accounts for multiple administrations in a single organization.

The CDI assesses the full organization against the six symptoms of attachment. The tool is truly a *diagnostic* tool to discover which symptoms emerge within an organization. It is best used when focusing on where there may be challenges to address, not over analyzing the data within the CDI for a single organization. Having said that, we want to share some of the data to provide a flavor of this is the case. The CDI is reported on a 1 to 5 scale for an overall rating and then a 1 to 5 scale for each of the six symptoms. Over 10 years of 18,000 responses, the CDI yields the following results for organizations:

The way to interpret results is that a higher number means there is a symptom that needs attention within an organization. Now remember, each symptom is reported on a 1 to 5 scale and a higher score indicates a symptom that may need attention. So, in most organizations the symptoms are not presenting strong numbers that vary from the norm (roughly 3 on the scale). The overall score across all organizations is 2.24 out of 5, which is why the numbers themselves provide little value. However, in almost every organization individual symptoms provide some instructive guidance for the organization or even divisions within an organization (when administered in a large organization).

Our analysis of the total set of 18,000 responses reveals two interesting lessons about how organizations get Stuck. First, increases in the first four symptoms tend to lead to increases in the last two. In Table 7.2, we highlighted the first four symptoms of Loss of Productivity, Morale, Motivation, and Conflict in contrast with the last two of Absenteeism and Turnover. This is because our research demonstrates a time-bound link between the symptoms. Over time, as the first four increase, it leads to an increase in both Absenteeism and Turnover. In particular, there is a strong correlation between the Loss of Productivity and the two symptoms of Absenteeism and Turnover. This makes sense intuitively, too. If you feel

TABLE 7.2

CDI Distribution from 2011 to 2020

Overall CDI Score	2.24
Loss of Productivity	1.84
Morale	2.74
Motivation	2.08
Conflict	1.99
Absenteeism	1.76
Turnover	1.72

a Loss of Productivity, it may slow your willingness to engage. This in turn leads to Absenteeism and the likelihood of seeking a new role.

Second, in over 95 percent of the administrations, Morale is the top symptom for the organization as a whole. In the rare cases where Morale is not the top issue, it is very close, with Motivation winning out. One rare case was where the organization was struggling with deep Conflict leading to intense issues of Productivity, Motivation, and Turnover. This challenge goes deeper as Morale is the top symptom for 65 percent of the individual respondents, we have encountered over the last 10 years. We know both anecdotally and through research that Morale is highly correlated with leadership. The challenge of leadership in organizations is a significant driver as to why Morale continues to emerge in the CDI. Yet, we also know the critical role that leadership plays in develop and supporting people through the process of becoming Unstuck. Much more on leadership later in Chapter 8.

Our team administers the CDI across many industries. In particular, there are a high number of respondents in education, consulting, and health care organizations. Overall we observe lower levels of attachment symptoms in educational organizations with significantly higher symptoms in consulting organizations. In consulting organizations in particular, Morale is a strong area of concern. Health care organizations have historically sat between the educational and consulting organizations, but we have not been able to observe any data during the pandemic, when we hypothesize these symptoms might be more likely to reveal themselves.

The response to these symptoms varies for each organization based on the leaders, the results, and the situation. No two organizations are the same. Sometimes the CDI identifies the people challenges in an organization ahead of a new agenda. For example, a new leader within a global defense organization used the CDI to understand the landscape across his organization. The survey was administered across 35 countries in both English and Spanish, and coupled with many in-depth interviews to round out the quantitative analysis. The leader considered a restructuring and realignment of the entire organization. The CDI revealed that unclear expectations across the organization was contributing to low Morale, blurred lines of responsibility were reducing Motivation, and a weak organizational identity was creating Conflict within the organization and with external partners. As a result, the leader did move forward with his restructuring, but focused on re-invigorating the Mission of the organization, not just the efficiency of its people.

Sometimes the CDI helps identify that the people are not the challenge, but it is the technology or the solution that needs to be addressed. For example, an early use of the CDI with a pediatric practice revealed relatively good scores for all participants in the organizations with one exception. The nurses reported a Loss of Productivity. They had no other attachment symptoms, but the Loss of Productivity was astonishing high. The team dug in with some follow-up conversations and found that the technology was creating a significant amount of new work for them. It was literally reducing their productivity. They liked it, they were positive, it was just slowing them down. From the findings, we were able to help the development team adjust the workflows and fix the clunky solution to a more streamlined approach. In the end, what may have seemed like resistance was a technical concern easily solved within weeks.

In another healthcare organization, the CDI helped identify that while the organization recognized the need to change, the organization lacked a shared understanding of the path forward. Overall, the organization appeared to be change ready. The only symptom of concern was Morale, which was relatively low, and the other symptoms were equally low. However, the qualitative questions revealed that the team lacked common understanding of two key elements: 1) the process for change going forward and 2) what change solution would work for the organization. This led the research team to a different conclusion than usual. This group wasn't Stuck because in their minds, a change had not started yet.

ATTACHMENT SYMPTOMS AND THE U.S. FEDERAL GOVERNMENT

Each year, the United States federal government administers a survey through the Office of Personnel and Management to nearly 1.4 million federal employees to understand overall employee engagement. The survey is called the Federal Employee Viewpoint Survey or FEVS.[2] The survey has been issued biannually since 2002 and annually since 2010. There are two great features of the survey. First, because it is the entire federal government, it has a scale that is hard to attain with any other organization. Second, despite this scale, it is not really one organization. The survey includes the civilian workforce for the 15 formal departments of the U.S. government and nearly 200 separate agencies. Each agency is a separate organization, ripe for analysis.

Within this survey, we found a set of questions that closely mirror the core questions of the Change Diagnostic Index©. In 2016, we began applying the CDI methodology to the FEVS data at both the macro-level of the federal government and at the agency level. We wanted to understand: (1) whether the methodology could translate easily and (2) whether the approach would be instructive. The results were more than instructive, they were insightful and powerful.

From 2010 to 2019, the FEVS survey included more than 5 million respondents from across the federal government. In total, the survey provided over 1,000 separate cases of organizations with enough sample size to review the results against the CDI metrics. We found similar, but slightly different patterns acrossthe U.S. federal government:

- While Morale is a top symptom in many agencies, it is not the top symptom across the agencies. In the government, Motivation and Conflict present as bigger symptoms of attachment.
- Respondents report symptoms of Absenteeism and Turnover more regularly in the federal government than in the other organizations we have observed.
- Leadership is even more highly correlated with Morale in the federal government than in our overall database, but leadership is also correlated with Conflict (more in a moment).

- The Mission of the government is a major driver of attachment and associated symptoms – when something questions or triggers the Mission, it can have an impact on the overall symptoms of the employees.
- External events have a significant impact on the attachment symptoms in the organization – public attention (positive and negative), issue salience, budgeting, scandal – all impact the symptoms of the employees, as well as internal change

The Value of Attachment Objects

We also found that the FEVS data let us test what objects people leaned on for support. Due to the wide range of questions available in the FEVS data, we were able to correlate the attachment symptoms with potential attachment objects that might be the cause of the symptoms and/or possible transitional objects for people. We identified five objects through the survey that we could assess – Mission, Senior Leaders, Direct Supervisors, Information, and Skills.

The Mission is a critical component of why many employees choose a job in the U.S. federal government over the private sector. Federal employees often feel a calling for the Mission-focused work they support. Across the board, we found that Mission is highly correlated with Morale, although not the top driver – that is still leadership. This is a critical intangible object that employees attach to, similar to the psychological contract, that drives behavior, attitudes, and sentiment across the government.

The results clarified the different roles that leaders play in the attachment process. The FEVS survey asks questions about both Senior Leaders (organizational leaders with who the respondent may not have direct interaction) and Direct Supervisors. The Senior Leaders are highly correlated with attachment symptoms of Morale, but the Direct Supervisors are not. On the other hand, Direct Supervisors are highly correlated with attachment symptoms of Conflict, while Senior Leaders are not. This makes sense intuitively that Direct Supervisors would have more direct control over Conflict in an employee's work situation, but it is somewhat surprising that employees would so clearly look to Senior Leaders for support around Morale.

Information and Skills both have an interesting role to play in the attachment process for federal employees. Both are highly correlated with Morale, Motivation, Conflict, and Turnover. Information presents a stronger correlation across all symptoms but is strongest with Conflict. When it comes to Motivation, Information is the strongest object to correlate with Motivation. This suggests that for U.S. federal employees, having Information to do their work is an important part of feeling motivated. While this finding is specific to the federal workforce, it is consistent with findings we have seen in other sectors.

Mission Matters: A Few Case Studies

We know that many U.S. federal employees take jobs with the federal government to support the Mission of the government – national security, public health, economic development, and so much more. The government sometimes offers slightly less financial compensation but affords employees the opportunity to make an impact on these crucial items that serve the broader society. In fact, for many employees, the Mission is an attachment they lean on to form a connection with their respective agency and support for the Mission is highly correlated with overall Morale across the federal workforce. What happens when that Mission changes?

For decades, children dreamed of working at NASA to go into space as part of the Space Shuttle program. In 2012, that program ended, and it changed the approach that many NASA employees took to their work. Instead of designing the transportation of the future, NASA would design programs with support from commercial companies. For many, this was a cataclysmic change. Others were more focused on the research in these programs and found that the research component of space exploration was all that mattered.

From 2010 to 2012, what we see in NASA is an initial decline in all the symptoms, perhaps as the reality of the 2012 Mission change becomes more real. Then from 2012 to 2019 there is a consistent positive shift in all the attachment symptoms. While Morale and Motivation were never that low to start, the more dramatic shifts were in Conflict and Turnover, which had an appreciably positive shift in the way the organization operated on a regular basis. And what correlated with the upward trend was a steady increase in support for the Mission (Figure 7.1). Even though the Mission changed, NASA employees began to buy-in to the new Mission and demonstrate resilience to the new agenda for the organization.

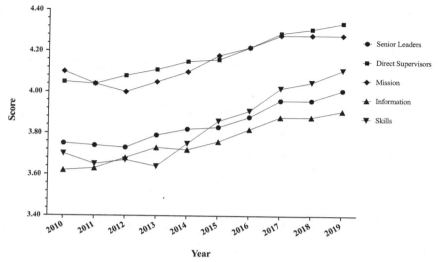

FIGURE 7.1
Attachment Objects in NASA, 2010–2019.

Similarly, other organizations display Morale and Motivation increases where there is overall issue salience around the Mission. The Centers for Medicare and Medicaid Services (CMS) received a significant shot in the arm during the early part of the 2010s. The agency received significant funding around the Affordable Care Act, which led to many new programs and responsibilities for the agency. The agency was charged with increasing access to health care via the healthcare.gov platform, but also increasing access to Information for the American people. As the issue of health care received attention and dollars came into CMS, the agency's scores increased and support for the Mission increased (Figure 7.2). We cannot be certain that the nation's interest in the Mission (via legislation and money) drove the increase in Morale, but there does seem to be a connection.

A more complicated case of Mission and attachment comes from Immigration and Customs Enforcement (ICE). Immigration in the United States is always a controversial topic. ICE sits at the heart of the controversy as the agency charged with removing people from the U.S. who illegal entered the country. As the U.S. debates how to enforce the nation's laws, ICE can often be praised or condemned, depending on the U.S. president's agenda. President Barack Obama wanted to focus enforcement on only individuals with criminal records while pursuing comprehensive immigration

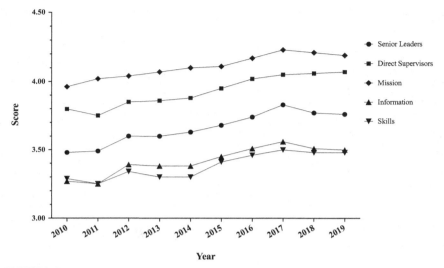

FIGURE 7.2
Attachment Objects in The Center for Medicare and Medicaid Services, 2010–2019.

reform. President Donald Trump wanted to provide more funding to ICE, remove more people from the country, and build a wall along the southwest U.S. border. Both of these presidential agendas had a direct impact on how the American people felt about the immigration system and ICE.

The FEVS data shows dramatic swings in all the attachment symptoms during this 10-year period. Starting in 2012, we start to see a steep decline in the scores for ICE Morale, Motivation, and Productivity. The attachment symptoms all suggest there is a strong sense of loss emerging in the organization. The highest overall symptom in ICE is Absenteeism, which is consistent across the period. When we look at the objects, we find that Mission is the most significant decline, along with Senior Leaders (those leaders at the top of the organization).

In 2016, we see that all these trends reverse. The attachment symptoms start to recover, and the objects move dramatically higher. By 2018, respondents report better scores on all symptoms and all the objects have better scores than then did in 2012 (Figure 7.3). For many in ICE, President Obama's agenda may have felt like a reduction of the Mission for ICE officers who were focused on enforcing the immigration laws of the country. This must have created a sense of loss. On the other hand, President Trump's agenda likely felt more like a full-throated endorsement of the agency after a few hard years of disagreeing with the presidential agenda.

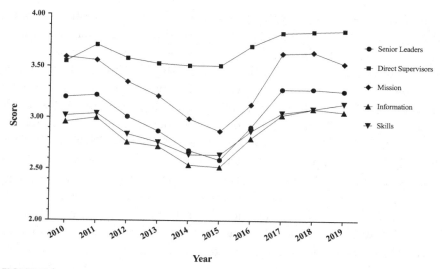

FIGURE 7.3
Attachment Objects in Immigration and Customs Enforcement, 2010–2019.

A noticeable and important baseline for the analysis is that support for Direct Supervisors did not waver over this entire period. This demonstrates two important factors. First, the unfortunate truth that Direct Supervisors can only control so much. Even though they are the primary contact point for so many people within an organizations daily work, there are many factors beyond their control. Second, the more hopeful reality that Direct Supervisors are a stabilizing force in an organization going through change and provide that sense of connection as many people feel a sense of loss to both the tangible and intangible items in their organization.

Bad Press Has an Impact

Sometimes, Morale and Motivation can be driven down by the negative attention an organization receives. Even if the behavior has nothing to do with the Mission, the attacks on the organization can drain the workforce and reveal the attachment to the organization. In 2012, the U.S. Secret Service scored in the of the FEVS "Best Places to Work" index. Morale was solid and employees were highly Motivated by their Mission, with the hallmark position of presidential protection. Nearly 8 in 10 agreed that "The agency is successful at accomplishing its mission."

By 2015, everything had changed. Morale plummeted, Motivation was down, and attrition had risen 12 percent in just three years. What happened? It started when there were reports that agents were propositioning prostitutes while on travel. This led to an investigation into travel practices that revealed several other incidents including intoxication on the job and protocol failures. The most public incident happened in 2014 when a fence jumper entered the White House before being encountered by Secret Service. It was the last straw. The Department of Homeland Security (DHS) brought in leadership from outside the agency.

In short, the Secret Service received poor management and it looks like the employee base could feel it. Starting in 2014, there was a steady decline in Motivation, Morale, and an increase in Conflict. All three continued until 2016 when new leadership was squarely entrenched. And starting in 2014, the same employee base started to report a decline in support for Senior Leaders who were driving the organization (Figure 7.4). Agents also seemed to feel the Information sharing lagged and Skills were declining over this period. All things that were later highlighted in the DHS report. But the employees of the Secret Service still stayed relatively attached to their Direct Supervisors, who were likely a source of comfort for most during these tumultuous times.

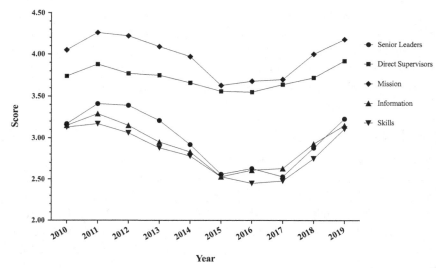

FIGURE 7.4
Attachment Objects in U.S. Secret Service, 2010–2019.

Likewise, similar trends hold in the case of the U.S. Patent & Trademark Office (USPTO) which saw significant shifts in Morale, Motivation, and Productivity because of managerial missteps over the last decade. The USPTO implemented a work-from-home policy in 1997 and it started with only 18 attorneys leveraging the program. In 2011, the policy was put into hyperdrive when the organization went to universal laptops. By the end of 2011, 83 percent of all eligible employees were teleworking.[3] Between 2010 and 2014, the employees reported dramatic increases in Morale, Motivation, Productivity, and a dramatic decrease in Conflict. Everything was good. Until...

In September of 2014, *The Washington Post* ran an article that a whistleblower had complained about the organization's telework policy and launched an investigation in 2012. The complaint became the Post's headline "Managers have no idea when their employees are working."[4] All the previous gains were erased over the next three years. Morale, Motivation, and Productivity dropped, while Conflict rose and the agency saw itself in the papers and on Capitol Hill with leaders accounting for the whistleblower's accusations.

Like the case of the Secret Service, the employee-base seemed to attach to their Direct Supervisors during this period (Figure 7.5). There was a decline is support for Senior Leaders and Information sharing, but the Direct Supervisors stayed relatively constant. Again, in this case the media attention did not seem to affect attitudes toward the Mission, like the case of ICE. This seemed to be a clear failure of leadership to manage the situation and the organization.

In these situations where there is media attention, it can be a tough balancing act for leadership. There is a need for action. However, the data shows that attachment symptoms are high in these situations, meaning that the employees are struggling with a sense of loss. The employee base may not be ready for immediate change because they have already clearly suffered, but that might be exactly what is necessary. While there is often a call for heads to roll, perhaps the most prudent and important thing to think about in these scenarios is how to balance the need for action with the need for attachment to the work at hand (the Mission). Even though the bad actors may need to be punished, the good performers will still be there. They will be attached to the work and their Direct Supervisors. They may be ready for what's next.

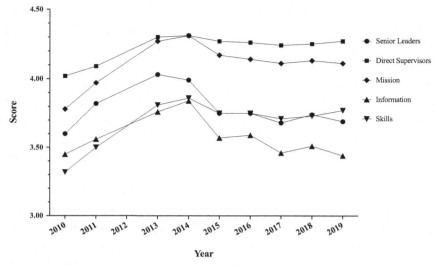

FIGURE 7.5
Attachment Objects in U.S. Patent & Trademark Office, 2010–2019.

The Value of Transition Objects

As we have seen in each of these cases, attachment objects provide a powerful tool for support within the organization. As we have seen in the case of Mission, when that intangible object is changed, that can be unsettling for an organization. On the other hand, we also see how other organizations can lean on Mission when other challenges arise. Likewise, we see how some organizations could have Senior Leaders "betray" the organization through bad leadership that let down the employees, while the Direct Supervisors provide support to the employee base to get them through the transition.

In this way, these attachment objects serve as both possible sources of loss and possible transitional objects to help employees through times of loss. Each of the five objects we tested has the potential to be a powerful transitional object during a turbulent time, if leveraged the right way. The key is to consciously think about these objects, the attachment they create, and how they can be used to move the organization through their current point, as outlined in Table 7.3.

TABLE 7.3

Common Transitional Objects

Transitional Object	Role of the Object
Senior Leaders	Drive initial messaging of change and connect staff with the reason the change is required
Direct Supervisors	Connect staff to their personal need for change, if trusted, and have the right Information to provide
Mission	Create an attachment to the Future State by creating an object or concept that will support the individual through the change
Information	Present open and honest Information to stakeholders throughout the change and once change is launched continue to communicate
Skills	Prepare all impacted employees with the right knowledge, Skills, and abilities to conduct their role/ function in the Future State

We know it is important to think about individual attachments. Organizational attachments add another layer of complexity to our challenge. We can identify when an organization is collectively demonstrating a sense of loss by looking at the symptoms demonstrated by the people in the organization. Many organizations go through a sense of loss when there is a change in the organization, others happen for external reasons (like issue salience). Whatever the reason, these diagnostics help us identify whether the people (and in turn the organization) demonstrate symptoms of loss and whether we need to develop interventions. The attachment objects and transitional objects help us identify what people lean on within the organization and what we may be able to help them leverage as they move beyond their current position and the organization becomes Unstuck.

PRACTICAL EXERCISES

COLLECT AND ANALYZE: IS YOUR ORGANIZATION STUCK?

To understand whether your organization is Stuck, you need to assess your organization against the attachment symptoms and determine where the challenges reside. The considerations below are NOT the Change Diagnostic Index. This is a not scientific tool, but it can quickly help you try to get a sense of where you might fall on attachment symptoms. Check off the boxes below (honestly) and see where you have the most challenges. This will help you start to think about where your organization is today.

Now, think about a change you are introducing or about to introduce. What will it do to some of these areas? Will it support areas of strength or challenge areas of weakness? Might it hinder overall Morale and Motivation? How? Could it reduce Productivity? How? What are the opportunities for Conflict? Might the change lead to Absenteeism or Turnover?

These questions in Table 7.4 should help focus your efforts and build solutions to help your organization get Unstuck.

TABLE 7.4

Change Diagnostic Considerations

Symptom	Considerations
Productivity	Do people in your organization tend to like the work they do? Do employees in your organization tend to think that the work they do is important?
Conflict	Do supervisors tend to listen to what employees say in the organization? Do employers within your organization effectively handle interpersonal issues with employees?
Motivation	Are employees given tangible opportunities to improve their Skills through a variety of learning channels (online, in-person, self-paced)? Do employees tend to get promotions in the organization or unit based on merit?
Morale	Do employees in the organization tend to have the feeling of personal accomplishment? Do supervisors know how to motivate employees in the organization and get a high-level of commitment on important initiatives?
Absenteeism	Are employees in the organization willing to put in the extra time and energy to get the job done? Do employees tend to miss or skip work on a regular basis?
Turnover	Do people in your organization generally recommend the organization as a good place to work for others? Has there been a high degree of turnover in the last 6–9 months?

ANALYZE: MISSION MATTERS?

Does the Mission matter in your organization? In this chapter we offered a few examples of where the Mission drives the overall attachment to the organization. We saw the same behavior in Chapter 4 with employees at Genentech. Think about the Mission for your organization:

- How do you define the Mission of your organization?
  - Do you define it based on the outcomes of the company?
  - Do you define it based on the outcomes of your customers or clients?
- To what degree is success anchored to the Mission?
  - Do performance metrics anchor mostly to the Mission?
  - Do performance measures anchor mostly to financial outcomes?
- How do different stakeholder groups respond to the Mission?
  - Leaders?
  - Employees?
  - Potential employees?
  - Customers?
  - Suppliers?
  - Business partners?
- If you are going to make a major change in the organization, do you need to consider the Mission?
- Based on how you answered the questions above, do you think that the Mission is an attachment object for your workforce?

NOTES

1 Grady, J., Grady, V., McCreesh, P., and Noakes, I. (2020). *Workplace Attachments: Managing Beneath the Surface.* New York: Routledge, p. 50.
2 The data for this section is based on the Federal Employee Viewpoint Survey (FEVS) conducted by the Office of Personnel Management (www.opm.gov/fevs/). The FEVS survey is administered annually and all of the data files can be collected from the period

reviewed here: www.opm.gov/fevs/public-data-file/. The questions from FEVS were aligned to the questions from the CDI and then assessed over the full period.

3 "2011 Telework Annual Report." United States Patent and Trademark Office. Accessed electronically on July 3, 2021 at:www.uspto.gov/sites/default/files/about/offices/cao/ TeleworkAnnualReport2011-508.pdf.

4 Rein, L. (2014). "Patent Office Whistleblower: 'Managers have no idea when their employees are working'" *The Washington Post.* September 12, 2014. Accessed electronically on July 3, 2021 at: www.washingtonpost.com/news/federal-eye/wp/2014/ 09/12/patent-office-whistleblower-managers-have-no-idea-when-their-employees-are-working/.

8

Leading a Stuck Organization

"If you want to make enemies, try to change something."

Woodrow Wilson

"People are very open-minded about new things, as long as they're exactly like the old ones."

Charles F. Kettering

Aris Scarla is not your average civil servant. He has served over 25 years in the Federal Aviation Administration (FAA). He started his career as an inspector and continued to grow through the ranks of the agency as a manager, leader, and an agent for change. In 2014 Aris was charged with creating a Change Management Program for the Flight Standards Service. He was dedicated to building a capability for change within the FAA. Aris engaged leaders in active conversation about the role they would play in change, he rolled out change management training to more than 4,500 employees across the Flight Standards Services, and he developed activation strategies to support the team members as they went to implement change management programs.

By 2019, Aris was deep into the implementation of the FAA's *Workforce of the Future Initiative*. Unfortunately, Aris continued to hit a familiar challenge. The well-trained advisors in his cohort couldn't get people to adopt the change no matter how hard he tried. There was a gap between understanding what they needed to do and their desire to change. In 2019, Aris decided he needed to study this gap and understand how to close it. He assembled a research team that leveraged the Attachment Styles Index to target his front-line leaders and managers. The response rate to the survey was good and he was confident the tool would provide him insights to support his program.

DOI: 10.4324/9781003157458-8

The assessment revealed that overall, the breakdown of individuals attachment styles was close to what we would expect with 84 percent of cohort Stable, 7 percent Distracted, 2 percent Autonomous, and 5 percent Insecure. While this is consistent with other organizations, there is no right attachment style. In fact, such a high number of Stable individuals can create a challenge in an organization as Stable individuals are often blind to the challenges of others. Stable individuals often discount or are unaware of the change impact on those individuals in the organization who are **not** securely attached. Given that this cohort were front-line leaders and managers, it is likely that the workforce itself was not Stable. In short, his leaders may have isolated his employees.

The assessment also revealed some uncertainty about the program itself. Only 61 percent of the front-line leaders understood the vision for the change effort and barely half agreed that there would be benefits from the new program (52 percent). These leaders were essential for the success of the change initiative, yet many did not understand why they were doing it and most felt there was no benefit. How could Aris expect them to have a desire for change? Worse, what kind of message were they sending to the people that worked for them?

The team developed three tactical adjustments with Aris that his team could begin immediately:

1. Develop a translation process for leadership vision at the operational level.
2. Test the messages in areas of the organization where cultural differences are known to exist.
3. Coach the leadership to strategically communicate the change message without imposing a secure attachment message.

As we fast-forward to 2021, we have seen the Flight Standards' program succeed and become a model for other programs in the federal government. Not only did Aris rollout the program across Flight Standards, he developed a position description for the FAA and he developed a government-wide position description for a change advisor. When the FAA set out to build the change management program, the goal was to be the "Gold Standard" and Aris believes that's exactly what he has built.

Like so many people driving change, Aris found that leadership was a critical factor in the success of the FAA's program. He needed his leaders to be engaged in the right way with the right understanding of the change effort to drive success. In its biannual study of change practitioners, the research and training organization Prosci® consistently finds that change practitioners report that "Active and Visible Sponsorship" is the number one success factor in change management efforts.[1] When leaders understand the change they sponsor and can actively engage to advocate and mobilize for it, then change efforts succeed. Of course, this assumes the leaders can effectively connect with the organization that is Stuck.

In this chapter we will explore:

- How do attachment styles impact the relationship between leaders and followers?
- How do these relationships shift during times of change?
- How should we rethink change management for Stuck organizations?
- How does this impact the way leaders behave during times of change?

Leadership is a complex topic. At any given point you can walk down the aisle of your average airport bookstore and find a dozen new products telling you how to "lead today." Bernard Bass developed the comprehensive *Handbook on Leadership* that recounts in more than 1,500 pages of encyclopedic reference the thousands of studies completed on the topic of leadership over the decades. As Bass notes, the leader:

- Helps set and clarify the missions and goals
- Energizes and directs others to pursue the missions and goals
- Helps provide the structure, method, tactics, and instruments for achieving the goals
- Helps resolve conflicting views about means and ends
- Evaluates the individual, group, or organizational contribution to the effort

Most importantly, leadership today is a relationship between the leader, the follower, and the situation. A leader needs to provide all the skills that Bass outlines above, while aligning the expectations and motivations of the followers in the organization against the situation at hand. For this process to work, the leader must be able to connect with the follower and create a strong relationship. We have found that attachment styles provide a good signal to the type of relationship a leader and follower can develop.

THE LEADER–FOLLOWER RELATIONSHIP

To understand the relationship between a leader and follower, we must study the leader, the follower, and the relationship. This requires creating four separate units of study – the unique attributes of the leader, the unique attribute of the follower, the leader's view of the follower, and the follower's view of the leader. This relationship is often described as a dyad. The attributes of the leader and the follower are best represented with the Attachment Styles Index (as discussed in Chapter 4). The relationship is measured using a tool called the Leader-Member Exchange (LMX) Questionnaire (example in the Practical Exercises), which allows us to determine what attributes have the strongest impact on the relationship between a leader and a follower. From this approach we can learn a great deal about different types of leaders with different types of followers in different types of situations.

As way of a reminder, the four attachment styles are: Stable, Autonomous, Distracted, and Insecure. Conventional wisdom suggests that Stable individuals make the best leaders due to their secure base and balance. However, Stable leaders can also be blind to the challenges of other people, especially in times of change. This can make Stable leaders off-putting to followers who are not Stable. On the other hand, leaders with Distracted style can be effective with all types of followers. These individuals are less likely to be blind to the challenges of others and demonstrate some of their own weaknesses. On the other hand, in a situation of Distracted follower with a Stable leader, the follower is more likely to give a positive LMX score to the leader than the other way around. This is likely due to the nature of the Distracted individual's low avoidance and high need for connection.

Autonomous leaders and followers are more likely to provide negative feedback on the other part of their relationship (leader or follower) regardless of which position they hold. However, Autonomous leaders receive better ratings from followers than leaders with more anxiety, likely due to their more hands-off approach. Individuals with difficulty regulating emotions, such as highly Distracted or highly Anxious individuals may struggle as leaders, especially during times of change when stress may bring out their worst tendencies to self-regulate their anxiety. However, as any Attachment Style intensifies, the negative qualities of the style tend to outweigh the positive strengths of the style.[2]

The core of this concept is understanding the attributes of the leader and the follower to understand the relationship. Of course, each relationship (dyad) will be completely different. However, this approach does help both the organization and the leader start to focus on the attributes of the people involved instead of pre-conceived expectations of how people should behave. As Brene Brown notes,

> Leading for true belonging is about creating a culture that celebrates uniqueness. What serves leaders best is understanding your 'players' best efforts. My job as a leader is to identify their unique gift or contribution. A strong leader pulls players toward a deep belief in themselves.[3]

Leader–Follower Relationships in Times of Change

Attachment styles can have a major impact on how individuals react to change. In the leader-follower relationship, these impacts will be intensified when both parts of the relationship feel the impact at the same time. As individuals, Stable leaders should handle change well, while Distracted leaders may become excessively reliant upon others through change. Autonomous and Insecure people may tend to avoid change, which could create a challenge for both the organization and their followers. Organizations may not get the advocacy and/or sponsorship they need, whereas followers may not get the information and support they need.

As followers, Stable individuals should adapt well to effectively managed change. Distracted people can effectively handle change if the leader provides resources to help them through change. Autonomous and Insecure followers may struggle through change due to their low expectations and distrust of others.

Of course, the goal is to align leaders and followers more effectively at the relationship level. To that end, MaryJo Kolze, a George Mason Ph.D. candidate, has been working diligently to develop a view of how each Attachment Style interacts with the others during change. Table 8.1 represents the culmination of her very deep analysis in this space:

TABLE 8.1

Leader–Follower Relationships Based on Attachment Style in Times of Change

	Leader is Stable (Secure)
Follower is Stable (Secure)	Matched Styles. Mutual resilience through change. Mutual high expectations through change. Change should (relatively) not be an issue except for challenges related to blind spots and/or lack of empathy.
Follower is Autonomous (Dismissive)	Follower avoids change and disengages due to low expectations for others. Leader is resilient to change and doesn't see why follower has disengaged / avoided change. Leader may not recognize why follower is upset and have little tolerance for it. This may fulfill follower's low expectations of the leader and of the change process. Change may not go well for this pair and may result in further damage to the relationship.
Follower is Distracted (Preoccupied)	Follower is stressed through change and may seek extra validation from the leader. Leader is resilient to change and doesn't understand why follower has become so needy through change. If the leader has social regulation, time, and resources to provide needed validation, this may go well. If leader lacks social regulation, time, or resources to provide needed validation to follower, change may be too much for the follower to handle, which could severely demotivate the follower.
Follower is Insecure (Fearful)	Follower is mistrustful of those close to him / her, and this is exacerbated during change. Follower appears withdrawn from change, actively avoids change, and suppresses their reactions when around others. Leader is resilient to change and may not pick up on follower's negative reactions or doesn't understand why follower is more mistrustful than normal. This can result in damaged relationship but may not appear to have anything to do with the change.
	Leader is Autonomous (Dismissive)
Follower is Stable (Secure)	Follower is resilient and comfortable with change. Leader is avoidant of change, which may result in followers experiencing unnecessary time pressure to engage in change (if leader stalls). If follower found out about "unnecessary" stalling / avoidance on the part of the leader, this could result in distrust of the leader going forward, but would likely not result in a poor change process.

TABLE 8.1 CONT.

Leader–Follower Relationships Based on Attachment Style in Times of Change

Follower is Autonomous (Dismissive)	Matched styles. Mutual low expectations for others through change. Both may avoid change until it absolutely has to be dealt with. However, due to low expectations for others change may end up well when both finally are forced to deal with it. Mutual understanding of avoidance of change.
Follower is Distracted (Preoccupied)	Follower is stressed through change and may seek extra validation from the leader. Leader is avoidant of change and has low expectations for others, so will likely not be able to provide the needed validation. For an avoidant leader high in empathy, this could end up as a great situation in which helping the follower forces the leader to engage with change. For an avoidant leader low in empathy, this could end very poorly as follower is not supported through change and leader continues to avoid more and more strongly.
Follower is Insecure (Fearful)	Follower is mistrustful of those close to him / her, and this is exacerbated during change. Leader is avoidant of change as well, with low expectations of others. This will likely result in the team as a whole reacting poorly to and avoiding change for compounding reasons.
	Leader is Distracted (Preoccupied)
Follower is Stable (Secure)	Follower is resilient and comfortable with change. Leader is able to understand and support followers and is reassured by follower resilience. Good outcomes expected here.
Follower is Autonomous (Dismissive)	Follower avoids change and disengages due to low expectations of others. Leader understands follower's avoidance, which undermines leader's confidence. If leader receives validation from another source, leader can act in engaging ways to support follower despite low expectations and avoidance. If leader does not receive validation from another source, he / she may play into follower's low expectations through inaction.
Follower is Distracted (Preoccupied)	Matched styles. Mutual high connection and understanding of how others feel. Both may feel insecure and need reassurance to engage with change, but both may also rise to the occasion to provide that support.

(*continued*)

TABLE 8.1 CONT.

Leader–Follower Relationships Based on Attachment Style in Times of Change

Follower is Insecure (Fearful)	Follower is mistrustful of those close to him / her, and this is exacerbated during change. Leader understands follower's mistrust and likely reasons for mistrust, which undermines leader's confidence. If leader receives validation from another source, leader can work to slowly gain follower trust and encourage the change process. If leader does not receive validation from another source expect inaction.
	Leader is Insecure (Fearful)
Follower is Stable (Secure)	Follower is resilient and comfortable with change. Leader is mistrusting and will likely withdraw from the change process. Follower will be left to fend for him / herself during change but will likely be okay anyway. Follower will not be understanding and may result in damaged relationship with leader.
Follower is Autonomous (Dismissive)	Follower avoids change and disengages due to low expectations of others. Leader is mistrusting and will likely withdraw from the change process. Leader actions will align with low expectations from followers. Tendency to avoid change to the extent possible. Long-term relationship damage not expected due to fulfilled expectations.
Follower is Distracted (Preoccupied)	Follower is stressed through change and may seek extra validation from the leader. Leader is mistrusting and withdrawn, and therefore unlikely to provide needed validation to follower. Excess relationship seeking on the part of follower pushes leader into further withdrawal. Excess withdrawal on the part of leader further demoralizes and demotivates follower. Not recommended.
Follower is Insecure (Fearful)	Matched styles. Mutual mistrust exacerbated through change. Expect each individual to seclude themselves to the extent possible through change, rather than acting in relationship. Tendency to withdraw from and avoid change to the extent possible.

An understanding of the leader-follower relationship based on Attachment Style provides us a few key lessons for change:

- ***Don't just focus on the leader.*** Too often, change assessments focus on leader traits and styles. It is far more important to focus on the alignment of the leader and the followers in the change effort. The traits of the followers are just as important as the traits of the leaders. There are more followers, and we need them to adopt the change!

- **Assess the ability to modulate (Attachment) Style.** Organizations often ask leaders to modulate their style based on the situation. However, leaders also need to learn to address different types of attachment styles. As leaders mature in organizations, they need to be able to create both awareness and deep understanding of different attachment styles and how to lead these different styles.
- **Create some relationship, even informal.** It is possible to create better alignment of leaders and followers to work through periods of change. While it may not be possible to align each person to the perfect formal leader, there are ways to create better leadership structure. This might be done through informal groups of support or through more formal coaching discussions to ensure that critical team members get the support they need during a change effort.
- **Comfort yields comfort.** When many followers in a group effectively align to leaders based on attachment style, it should have a positive effect on the entire group's adoption of the change. While we have not had the chance to demonstrate this in a setting yet, it stands to reason that the flywheel effect will cause more comfort within the group.

HOW TO UNSTICK AN ORGANIZATION

Building on our story, we now know how people get Stuck, how organizations get Stuck, how to assess the symptoms of an organization looking to move forward, and how to assess leaders and followers. Now, the critical question is – How do we Unstick an organization? Or more, accurately, how do we help people within an organization who are Stuck move from the Current State to the Future State. There is an entire discipline around this function called Change Management. For those of you unfamiliar with the discipline, change management supports people with the usage and adoption of new organizational initiatives – leaders, strategies, process, technologies, and, well, anything. We do not plan to revisit the discipline in this section. There are many great works on the subject.[4]

Our goal in this section is to demonstrate how our research on the brain and attachment helps move organizations that get Stuck. We want to demonstrate some minor adjustments to change management concepts that can build a better approach to change. The key to success is bringing the brain to the party. A stronger focus on the Intuitive Brain and the attachment process will build better solutions to support people in their individual response to change. Instead of thinking about resistance to change, we must reframe the conversation to the biological function of attachment and then respond with techniques that account for the lessons of attachment.

Rethink Change Management

In general, Change Management programs follow a similar path:

- Clearly identify the change
- Develop a leadership team around the change
- Develop a strategy to engage the impacted stakeholders
- Implement the strategy with effective communications and training
- Develop performance measures to ensure that stakeholders continue the new behavior.

This is a perfectly fine process for change management. Many organizations have put their own proprietary spin on the approach and have developed unique tools and models to support the approach. The professional organization, the Association of Change Management Professionals (ACMP) has developed a detailed Standard for Change Management© that provides a broadly accepted view of the process that is publicly available for consumption. We are both founding members of ACMP, supporters of the organization, and designed a training program around the Standard for Change Management©.

There are two problems with these process-focused models of Change Management. First, they seem to focus more on the process than on the brain of the people involved in the change. One thing that sits at the heart of all of these models is the underlying challenge that organizational change still happens one person at a time. No matter the size of the organization, there is a need to move each person through a change process. They must be willing to let go of their Current State and connect with the Future State.

Many of the process-focused models simply obfuscate the individual perspective within their process. The process itself becomes the end with a connection formed to the process, rather than the outcome of change.

Second, Change Management is not working. Well, it is not working as well as we would like. A seminal 2000 article claims that Change Management efforts fail 70 percent of the time. This is probably inaccurate and certainly outdated. Mark Hughes and many others have explained the reasons this number is flawed.[5] But the bigger question is – why are we having that debate? With an increasing number of change practitioners around the globe, thousands trained in the discipline, dedicated undergrad and grad programs on the discipline, and even new positions in the public and private sector dedicated to Change Management – why is there a debate about the success? *Because it is not working.*

Change Management as a process-focused industry is not meeting the brain. Change Management as a people-focused discipline can. As John Kotter notes:

> The world basically uses change management, which is a set of processes and a set of tools and a set of mechanisms that are designed to make sure that when you do try to make some changes – A) it doesn't get out of control, and B) the number of problems associated with it – you know, rebellion among the ranks, bleeding of cash that you can't afford – doesn't happen. So it is a way of making a big change and keeping it, in a sense, under control.[6]

Change must change. Change Management should not be about "keeping control," but should be about supporting people through the adoption of new initiatives in an organization. Any change effort needs to focus on four key questions:

- Why is the organization changing?
- How do stakeholders need to change their behavior?
- Why should stakeholders want to change?
- What do we need to do to avoid them falling into old behavior?

Instead of developing more complex processes to think about managing change, organizations can simplify the approach by answering these questions and supporting the people with brain-driven tools. There are five areas that we need to enhance if we want organizations to become Unstuck:

- Leadership
- Communications
- Training
- Performance Management
- Transitional Objects

Rethink Leadership for the Stuck Organization

In our aggregate examination of the CDI, we saw that Morale is the most common attachment symptom observed in organizations across all sectors quickly followed by Motivation. These symptoms both point to challenges with leadership in the organizations we studied. But it is not just in organizations that took the CDI. Within the FEVS data, we see the same challenge. Over the last 10 years, we see a consistent trend on questions about leadership. Scores for Senior Leaders have remained relatively constant over the years, while scores for Direct Supervisors have gone up modestly. And we know that Morale is linked to Senior Leaders, while Motivation is linked to Direct Supervisors. Against this backdrop, how does an organization attempt to move its people forward through the challenges of today to a brighter future?

Identify the Loss

Each person has different attachments. For some it might be to people, but for others it might be to physical objects in their space. Leaders and managers can effectively work through all these adjustments by engaging with team members to understand what they miss. This can be a group conversation or leaders can do these conversations one-on-one. The core of the conversation is to identify what people might be missing to understand how to support them through any of these challenges. The conversation may start with, "When you think about how we are changing, what are you missing?" The answers may be surprising. It could be as big as the psychological contract or as small as an object on their desk. You never know!

Design Attachment-Based Leadership Profiles

The first step is to acknowledge that leadership is not a function, but a relationship. Like the psychological contract we discussed in Chapter 5, leadership rests on an unspoken pact between the leader and the followers. As we described above, leaders can become more effective at understanding and managing different types of attachment styles. Over time, organizations can develop profiles of leaders that track whether the Attachment Style Index assessment and the results align. For example, has the Distracted leader been effective at managing the change efforts placed in front of her? Additionally, these profiles can used to understand where development needs to occur for leaders in the future.

Think of Leaders As Attachment Objects

The second step is to acknowledge that the leader is more than just a person. The leader is also a representation of the past memory, emotion, and learning that an employee has developed with the organization and likely before the organization. This means that there is great strength in aligning the right leader to the right situation at the right time, but there is also great risk of removing the right leader at the wrong time. This leads to a few points of practical guidance:

- Be intentional about leader selection, leader alignment, and leader removal; leverage tools like the ASI to ensure that leaders are being aligned to the right followers for the situation
- Analyze the loss of key leaders as completely as the loss of other assets in the organization: What are the connection points? Who is impacted? What are the relational gaps? Who is at risk? Who needs support?
- Build a networked approach to leadership that moves beyond a single hierarchical line of leaders and mitigates the risk of relational loss in organizations to provide broad-based support networks for talented individuals

Diversify Leadership Roles and Expectations

Leadership provides different roles in the attachment process at different levels of the organizations. As we saw in the FEVS data, a Senior Leader supports Morale in the organization, whereas a Direct Supervisor connects more with Motivation and the management of Conflict. These findings are instructive in how we think about and leverage leaders in our organizations:

- Senior Leaders need to drive the vision of the organization and in times of change connect the change to the vision
- Senior Leaders need to set the tone – while each leader will find their own balance between positivity and authenticity, the tone needs to be appropriate to the leader, the situation, and the followers
- Direct Supervisors can guide employees through messaging about the organization's direction and any changes coming with tailored emphasis on the employee; they can be the trusted voice
- Direct Supervisors need training in conflict management; often Direct Supervisors are brought into the role of manager without an understanding of conflict management and yet this is a major symptom that emerges when employees feel loss
- Direct Supervisors need relevant, timely, and complete information on the organization if they are going to motivate their employees and provide stability in the organization

Rethink Communications Programs

Our research on attachment theory has taught us three big lessons on communications in organizations:1) be honest, 2) be vivid, and 3) be heard. These may seem simple, but they can be hard to execute. Yet, this is the core of what our brain is looking for when we listen to communications. If we are trying to get people to change their behavior, we are asking them to let go of something in the Intuitive Brain, which means we need to access the Intuitive Brain:

- Any confusing language or deviation in message may get them trying to game out our logic
- Without vivid imagery, we may not hit that emotional or memory core we want
- Without thinking about how the recipient receives information, we may never be heard

With this in mind, we recommend rethinking communications in three ways.

Acknowledge the Loss

We both find ourselves telling clients that Change Management is not magic. We cannot help leaders hide what is happening in the company and make people look elsewhere. When there is a shift from a Current State to a Future State, many employees will feel a sense of loss. Organizations cannot sugar coat that, communications must acknowledge the loss. There is often a logical business reason for the change, and it will likely – fill in the blank (save money, make money, yield efficiency, yield effectiveness, create organizational strength) – but it will not be easy for everyone. The sooner and more regularly the communications acknowledge the loss, without harping on it and being negative, the more authentic and successful the program will be.

Develop the Storytelling

When we talk about making a change in an organization, we often talk about the business need for the change. Even the business need for the change can come with a compelling story. Here's why. Researcher Uri Hasson has demonstrated through a series of studies and one compelling Ted Talk how brains can "couple" through storytelling. Storytelling can bring together the two parts of the brain in a way that a standard presentation on business will not. Put that together with the part of the brain we are trying to impact (the Intuitive Brain), where we know that we need to hit memory or emotion, and there is little value in a traditional business case. If we want to unlock the Intuitive Brain, we need to share memories, not messages; tales instead of talking points.[7]

Diversify the Techniques for Active and Passive Communication

Often in an enterprise transformation there may be a broad-based communications program that will include a variety communications messages, mediums, and messengers. However, these variations may be oversimplified and may not get at the real differences in the organizational populations. Based on the work of Attachment Styles, we know that people respond to change in different ways. Some will actively seek support because they are looking for engagement with individuals (Distracted) or the organization (Stable). Others are more likely to withdraw into their echo chamber of self-examination and reflection (Autonomous) or concern (Anxious).

As a result, the communication techniques and mediums must be varied to meet these types. Logistically, this means creating town hall sessions and conference calls to answer in-depth questions for the Distracted/Stable, but also publishing the same information for the Autonomous/Anxious. It may mean offering coaching packets with detailed information for Direct Supervisors, but also giving supervisors the latitude to hand those materials over to employees who may not engage effectively in those conversations.

Rethink Training Programs

One of the keys to successfully moving an organization forward is training. As any new paradigm enters the organization, there is a need to train people on the shift. Whether it is a new strategy, a new process, a new leader, or a new technology; team members need to learn how to succeed in the Future State. This often means new skills. However, often, the skills are really a secondary objective to the new behaviors sought through the change program. Our collective research is instructive in rethinking training in three ways to focus more on re-learning behavior rather than simple skills training.

Build Desire through Training

Many Change Management approaches have a part of the model that focuses on the readiness, willingness, or the desire for change. This part sits at the beginning of the Change Management process, and it becomes a gate or a milestone which the program must pass before the initiative can move forward. For example, a statement may be made like, "We must assess the readiness for change, then communicate the need for the change in a way that makes the case for change at a business level. We will then make the individual case for change in a personal way. This will help build up the individual readiness, willingness, or desire for change. Then we will train them." It's wrong.

That is not the way our brain works. Our brain is not linear. As we have looked at the Intuitive Brain in this book, we have shown you that the Limbic System brings together memory, emotion, and learning in one place. Desire to change is an emotional process and for most people it cannot be overcome by logic and *voiced emotion* (e.g., a message of What's in it For Me). Instead, most people will need to *learn* the change to create the willingness to change. Habit-forming experts often tell people try something for 21 days to form the habit. The process of learning and forming new memories will form the emotional comfort with the change. Hearing is not believing, and neither is seeing – living it is believing.

Build Memories through Learning

Practically, programs focused on behavior change should prioritize training over communications. If it is a new technology an organization is rolling out, help people see the system – get hands on the keyboard. When they feel it, they will be more likely to understand the value and be more likely to adopt it. In addition to learning the skills and building an emotional connection with the new tool, they will be building memories that will reinforce the emotions and learning. For this reason, nothing beats the shared experience of classroom learning with colleagues. It may sound a little "old school," but it still works best because it takes all the other noise out of the equation. COVID notwithstanding, these types of environments create something completely new to share among a team of colleagues.

Gamify Learning

Some people love games, some people can't stand them. Regardless of what camp you fall into, there are two practical reasons to gamify learning programs. First, there is so much noise in organizations, that every change needs to break through with creativity. Games help get attention and mind space in the crowded field. Second, and more to the point of the research we presented here, is the transitional space. Games bring people out of their current space into a new space where they can learn and explore before trying to get them into a Future State. This transitional space is a very successful place for helping the brain re-wire and learn new skills and behaviors.

Rethink Performance Management

In many Change Management discussions, performance conversations make two common errors – they are ignored, or they are over complicated. If they are ignored, it is because the Change Management team believes that training and communications are Change Management. Wrong. Incentives change behaviors. Without strong incentives, new behaviors will backslide to comfortable old ones every time.

If performance management is overcomplicated, it is because the Change Management team becomes worried about demonstrating their "credit" for the effort compared to another team involved in the effort. Of course, these organizational dynamics are real and cannot be ignored. The reality is that there should be only one set of performance measures – those set out by the change effort. The real question is how to use research on the brain to roll out performance incentives differently and drive behavior change more effectively.

Make the Money Emotional

We know that cognitively encouraging individuals to change for monetary reasons is a very logic-based approach to change. It should work on its own. Often it doesn't because people struggle to understand what the money might mean. For example, telling someone that proper compliance with a new program will yield a one percent increase in the bonus pool means ... what exactly? However, messaging the same story as compliance with a new program will yield an average $3,200 for each person in the bonus pool or the equivalent of a cruise for two to the Bahamas suddenly plants a picture in the mind of what they might be working toward. Now, some may dismiss the image immediately, but they are likely to replace it with their own image because you have now encouraged them to think that way. That is no longer a monetary goal, it is an emotional goal.

Reward Intuitive Brain Milestones

Conversely, it is also advisable to reward behavior that sits in the Intuitive Brain. Instead of just rewarding the core outcomes of the change efforts, find ways to reward the efforts that support adoption and usage of the change effort. Those items that support change of memory, emotions, and learning behaviors. This might look like a spot reward to someone who successfully completes all the training programs for a new technology first. It might be an imagery contest where team members are invited to create visuals for a new strategy and a prize is awarded to the most effective overall visual. Or it might be a storytelling competition to build off the communications section above where an award is established for those who demonstrate the principles of a new values program effectively.

Although this sounds a little cheesy, all of these examples have been deployed in Fortune 500 companies over the last few years with significant success because they tie behavior change with emotional attachments and reinforce the behavior with real incentives.

Develop Transitional Objects

In Chapter 5, we discussed how individuals lean on objects throughout their life, but especially in periods of change. Transitional objects provide a critical support mechanism through change. In many cases, organizations develop transitional objects without realizing it. These objects serve as the bridge between a current object that someone leans on for support and a Future State where they do not need that object. In short, the object helps provide comfort or support through the period of loss.

The Power of Transitional Objects

Often project teams implementing a change will go to the corporate catalogue and order generic giveaway products for a project. This is a missed opportunity to *intentionally* identify a transitional object to support the individuals in the program through the change. In her first book, *The Pivot Point*[8], Victoria used the device of an allegory of a group of people during a storm to describe the role of attachment. For this group, she had the protagonist offer them a gift to be opened later. It turned out to be an empty box, but it didn't matter. They all kept it with them during the storm.

During a critical period of leadership loss on one of Patrick's projects, he provided his team a tactile device (or toy) called a Tangle®. He told them that the team would be losing a key leader and they had an opportunity to use the device during time of stress to both relieve their stress and think creatively about how to get through it. The goal was to get creative, not get Stuck. Patrick was telling this story in a crowd three years later and one of the team members still had the Tangle®.

The Transitional Person

There are many possible transitional objects, and each major change effort requires a transitional object that make sense for the effort. Sometimes the transitional object is a person. Often leaders play temporary roles in times of change, such as Change Champions or Change Agents, which is a wonderful way to create a transitional experience within a program. A trusted person in a key role provides a sense of familiarity to people, while also signifying a bridge between the past and the future. Identifying the right person is critical and depends on finding someone who is a connector that brings together people from many parts of the organization, which is required for successful adoption, *not just the loudest voice.*

The Transitional Object

The key is to identify an object that serves as a bridge to the mission or the people of the Current State, while supporting the change and the behavior of the Future State. In fact, as much as possible, the object should either directly encourage the person through the behavior change *or* support them with the loss of the change. For example, in an organization where a new time tracking system was being introduced, the transitional object was a giveaway during the promotional campaign that was a laptop camera cover with the new time tracking link on it. This was both a helpful giveaway and a subtle reminder of the change in behavior. There is a practical exercise at the end of this chapter that helps you develop your own transitional object.

Many organizations get Stuck because employees feel a sense of loss during a significant change effort. We can't keep up and we demonstrate our sense of loss through measurable and observable symptoms (Chapter 7). Organizations can do better for change efforts by more effectively aligning leaders and followers based on Attachment Styles to create a better sense of comfort through change. Leaders can do more to improve the process for employees through more effective Change Management that uses our full understanding of the brain to support our people. So often when leaders approach a change effort, they simply start from the wrong part of the brain. They start with the logical case for change first, but they fail to account for the Intuitive Brain. A rethinking of core Change Management functions with the addition of the Transitional Object will yield a more effective and more human approach to change. Don't start with logic, let's start with where things get Stuck.

PRACTICAL EXERCISES

APPLY: LEADER–FOLLOWER QUESTIONNAIRE

There are many versions of the Leader-Member Exchange Questionnaire. The version in Table 8.2 is inspired by the LMX 7 from Graen and Uhl-Bien.[9] This tool demonstrates how to apply the concepts in your own work. As a leader, you would answer this questionnaire about each person who reports to you. As a follower, you would answer this about your leader. Ideally, you will get both sides of the response and be able to compare the responses to better understand the relationship. For a leader with multiple followers, the leader will fill out many surveys, while each follower will fill out only one.

TABLE 8.2

Leader–Follower Survey

Question	1	2	3	4	5
How often do you know whether your leader/ follower is satisfied with your performance?	Rarely	Occasionally	Sometimes	Fairly often	Very often
How well does your leader/follower understand your daily challenges in the organization?	Not a bit	A little	A fair amount	Quite a bit	A great deal
How well does your leader/follower recognize your potential within the organization?	Not at all	A little	Moderately	Mostly	Fully
What is the likelihood of the leader/ follower to use the influence they have available to them to help with your workplace challenges?	None	Small	Moderate	High	Very High

(continued)

TABLE 8.2 CONT.

Question	1	2	3	4	5
What is the likelihood the leader/follower would directly engage with you to help you complete the tasks of your work?	None	Small	Moderate	High	Very High
I have enough confidence in my leader/follower to defend a decision even if he or she were not present to do so.	Strongly Disagree	Disagree	Neutral	Agree	Strongly Agree
How effective is your working relationship with the leader/follower?	Extremely Ineffective	Worse than Average	Average	Better than Average	Extremely Effective

 OBSERVE: SCORE YOUR ORG

Look at the areas Table 8.3 that are common functions in Change Management. How does your organization do on each of these areas from a zero (non-existent) to a five (perfect) score?

If you score something as a three or lower, review the recommendations in that section. What one item would you take and try to implement for your organization to make it more effective and more human?

TABLE 8.3

Score Your Org

Functional Area	0 (Non-existent) to 5 (Perfect)
Leadership	
Communications	
Training	
Performance Management	
Transitional Objects	

APPLY: BUILD THE BRIDGE – IDENTIFYING THE RIGHT TRANSITIONAL OBJECT

The purpose of this exercise is to help identify a transitional object that will support your organization through a change effort:

- Fold a piece of paper lengthwise and in half to create four boxes on the page:
  - In the upper left-hand corner label the box "Organization"
  - In the lower left-hand corner label the box "Change"
  - In the upper right-hand corner label the box "Emotion"
  - In the lower right-hand corner label the box "Behavior"

- When you think of the mission or the people of your organization, what comes to mind? What symbols, visuals, and physical things that represent the organization? Write the list in the Organization box.

- Next, think about the change or transformation that is about to happen for the people in the organization. When you think about the change itself, what kind of change is happening? Where in the organization is it happening?

- Third, think about the key emotional reactions you might get to the change. What do you expect to see? What do you want to see? What is the gap? What emotions do you need to see – Creativity, PLAY, or CARE?

- Last, think about the behavior that needs to change in the organization. What do people need to differently because of the change or transformation? How will their job change? Where will this happen? Will it be at their desk? Will it be somewhere else? A new physical location?

- Look at the lists you created and the items on them. What are the connection points across the four boxes? What are the common elements of the Organization and the Change? What about the behavior is new?

NOTES

1 "Best Practices in Change Management." *Prosci*. As accessed electronically on July 3, 2021 at: www.prosci.com/resources/articles/change-management-best-practices.
2 Fein, E. C., Benea, D., Idzadikhah, Z., and Tziner, A. (2020). "The Security to Lead: A Systematic Review of Leader and Follower Attachment Styles and Leader–Member Exchange." *European Journal of Work and Organizational Psychology, 29*(1), pp. 106–125.
   Kafetsios, K., Athanasiadou, M., and Dimou, N. (2014). "Leaders' and Subordinates' Attachment Orientations, Emotion Regulation Capabilities and Affect at Work: A Multilevel Analysis." *The Leadership Quarterly, 25*(3), pp. 512–527.
   Khorakian, A. and Sharifirad, M. S. (2019). "Integrating Implicit Leadership Theories, Leader–Member Exchange, Self-efficacy, and Attachment Theory to Predict Job Performance." *Psychological Reports, 122*(3), pp. 1117–1144.
   Mayseless, O. and Popper, M. (2019). "Attachment and Leadership: Review and New Insights." *Current Opinion in Psychology, 25*, pp. 157–161.
3 Brown, Brene. (2017). *Braving the Wilderness: The Quest for True Belonging and the Courage to Stand Alone*. New York: Random House, p. 108.
4 Aaron, S. and Nelson, K. (2008). *The Eight Constants of Change: What Leaders Need to Know to Drive Change and Win*. Dallas, TX: CornerStone Leadership Institute.
   Creasey, T. and Hiatt, J. (2012). *Change Management: The People Side of Change*. Loveland, CO: Prosci Learning Center Publications.
   Heath, C. and Heath, D. (2010). *Switch: How to Change Things When Change Is Hard*. New York: Currency.
   Kotter, John. (1996). *Leading Change*. Cambridge: Harvard Business School Press.
5 Beer, M. and Nohria, N. (2000). "Cracking the Code of Change." *Harvard Business Review, 78*(3), pp. 133–141.
   Hughes, Mark. (2011). "Do 70 Per Cent of All Organizational Change Initiatives Really Fail?" *Journal of Change Management, 11*(4), pp. 451–464.
6 Kotter, J. (2011). "Change Management vs. Change Leadership – What's the Difference?" *Forbes*. July 12, 2011. Accessed electronically on July 3, 2021 at: www.forbes.com/sites/johnkotter/2011/07/12/change-management-vs-change-leadership-whats-the-difference/?sh=660fa4d44cc6.
7 Haason, U., Ghazanfar, A., Galantucci, B., Garrod, S. and Keysers, C. (2012). "Brain-to-Brain Coupling: A Mechanism for Creating and Sharing a Social World." *Trends in Cognitive Sciences. 16*(2), pp. 114–121.
8 Grady, V. and Grady, J. (2013). *The Pivot Point: Success in Organizational Change*. New York: Morgan James.
9 Graen, G. B. and Uhl-Bien, M. (1995). "Relationship-Based Approach to Leadership: Development of Leader–Member Exchange (LMX) Theory of Leadership Over 25 Years: Applying a Multi-Level, Multi-Domain Perspective." *Leadership Quarterly, 6*(2), pp. 219–247.

9

Unsticking the Future

"Changing is what people do when they have no options left."

Holly Black

"An' here I sit so patiently
Waiting to find out what price
You have to pay to get out of
Going through all these things twice
Oh, Mama, is this really the end
To be Stuck Inside of Mobile with the Memphis Blues Again?"

Bob Dylan

Tim is a part of a team that designed a new technology. It is a lightweight suit you wear that helps improve your ability to lift extremely heavy objects, called an exoskeleton. The suit offsets part of the load to make lifting and bending tasks easier and safer. These devices hold great promise for warehouses and facilities, machinery, and repair roles (including military operations), and even health situations where there is long-term muscular degeneration. A powered exoskeleton can allow an average worker to lift over 200 pounds above their head, which means a worker in a warehouse can easily move around most products without the help of a forklift. And they can be as small a backpack. It is also big business with the market for exoskeleton suits estimated to reach $2.1 billion by 2026.

A large box store approached Tim's team and asked if it would be possible to develop a device that could keep their workers be safer while making the job easier and more efficient. Tim and the team developed an exoskeleton to do just that – make the job easier and safer. The store loved the product, but then came the rollout. The store wanted to hype it up. The marketing

DOI: 10.4324/9781003157458-9

team came up with the plan to rollout the suit using a comic book that played up the superhuman strength their warehouse team would get from the suit like Iron Man.

Tim hears the Iron Man comparison all the time. "The concept is right, but they will just be disappointed if that's what they get in their head. They really just need to feel it to understand." They used the approach in two stores and in two stores the staff was underwhelmed, some workers used the suits while others did not. They asked the workers "Who didn't use the suits and why?" The workers responded that they didn't want to be the center of attention or that they were "strong enough" and did not need "help" to do their job. The suits sat unused and the team was disappointed.

Then Tim had a different idea. Instead of hyping the suits, what if he undersold the suits? What if he just called them tools that fit like backpacks, Tim explained "If you can wear a backpack, you can use our exoskeleton." Tim tried this approach and it worked. The same workers who were initially reluctant, became users by trying out the "backpack." Over the next few months, the company changed their entire approach to adoption. Instead of telling people, they showed them. Instead of videos, they put backpacks on the people. No more comic book comparisons, it was real world experiences. No more superheroes, just super strength, safety, and sales.

Tim's story is common. A disruptive technology trying to connect with the market in the right way at the right time. He believed he had the right solution for a real problem, and he may be right; but if no one ever tried it, he would never know. The difference between a good idea and great product is often adoption. And the difference between adoption and resistance often comes down to the ability of the product to overcome the Intuitive Brain of the customer, employee, or leader. Often, they are Stuck.

Organizations today face much more than a simple decision about one solution. Each leader faces the challenges of multiple new technologies coming at them every day. Each new technology promises to revolutionize their business with efficiency and effectiveness never seen before. Add to the challenge that the demands of the workforce are shifting too. Our retiring workforce and our emerging workforce have very different needs with the new entrants seeking a type of social activism that requires leadership to rethink organizational engagement. All of this against the backdrop of a once in a century global pandemic that will change the way we work forever. Where will this take us?

This Chapter will explore:

- How do we Unstick digital transformation, automation, or analytics?
- How do we avoid getting Stuck in the post-pandemic world?
- How do we manage our multi-generational and diverse workforce with the right Stickiness?
- How do we avoid burnout without getting Stuck?
- What are five key takeaways for individuals, for leaders, and for organizations who are Stuck?

OUR CONSTANTLY CHANGING TECHNOLOGY

As much as we talk about a technology-driven economy, technological investments depend on people. The history of our global economy demonstrates a gradual process where we find balance between people and technology to create greater value as technology emerges to slowly improve the work of people. In each successive wave of economic evolution, we find that new technological solutions emerge, people slowly adopt, and organizations slowly adapt. While there is a trend over time that technology does have a displacement impact on certain roles in the economy, it is never as imminent nor as widespread as it may seem at the start of the new trend.

With the agrarian society, new techniques and large farming equipment slowly came to replace the individual farmer. Machines were introduced and gradually replaced many elements of the manufacturing supply chain. However, as the exoskeleton example shows above, machines have not replaced all parts of the supply chain. Emerging technology still looks to disrupt last mile delivery and the stocking of products. Many service jobs (like call centers) may be digitized over time, but higher order service jobs (like doctors and advisors) cannot be disrupted, and knowledge economy roles are the natural next step for those workers in the service economy.

Now, as we sit in the interaction economy, trends like digital transformation, increased automation, and data analytics again seem to threaten the human's role in economic production. But this change will not happen overnight. It will not be a clean cut to new technology. We will be in a state of transition for some time where humans and new forms of technology will need to collaborate for years to come. Moreover, this transition period of technology and human integration will require humans to adopt and use new forms of technology.

Digitally Transforming People

Digital transformation is the use of technology to strategically redesign the work of an organization. Often, organizations believe that digital transformation is the purchase of a new software or platform to manage a portion or all their business, but that is simply not the case. It is a holistic re-design of the business around a solution. Even the most robust platforms today – Salesforce, Workday, SAP – require significant process changes from the workforce to have a successful implementation. This simple difference in perspective immediately reveals the importance of people in digital transformation. There is simply no way to realize the value of a digital transformation without bringing people along for the journey.

Gerald Kane describes this as the technology fallacy. The technology fallacy is the mistaken notion that "because business challenges are caused by digital technologies, the solutions are also going to lie in digital technologies. The fact is that it is your people who will fuel – or thwart – your digital transformation." And through an extensive research program with surveys of 4,800 executives, managers, and employees from around the world over five years, Kane found … we are not ready. Only 44 percent of the more than 16,000 respondents in this study confirmed "their company is prepared for shifts in technology."[1]

The primary reason is that the shift is the technology fallacy. We need people to adopt before we are going to have a fully digital world and our people are not ready for this kind of change, so most digital transformations will be slow. To be clear, this is not a comment on the value of the solution or even the sales of the platforms. The platforms will sell. Leaders will buy them and try to implement them, but full value and true digital transformation will struggle without a complete understanding of the human side of the equation. Until organizations and leaders recognize the technology fallacy, digital transformation as a people-centered solution, the adoption of such solutions will struggle.

Augmented with Automation

The same is true with automation. Automation techniques like Robotic Process Automation (RPA) and ultimately Artificial Intelligence (AI) require humans. Many view these solutions as displacement strategies, but in reality, these solutions will spend many years working alongside humans to support the work of humans before these technologies will work autonomously from humans. Jason Kingdon, CEO of RPA leader Blue Prism, describes how the pandemic shined a light on the gaps existing between human workers and automation.[2] Kingdon likes to pitch companies that about half of all *tasks* for a digital worker (workers in the service or knowledge economy) can be accomplished by machines. The question remains whether machines can create the value that humans create in workflow through complex thought. These tasks should not be automated. Instead, automation should support workers in their *tasks* to be able to do more thinking and problem-solving toward more effective complex thought.

In a recent study of 1,300 CIOs and technology leaders, only 12 percent noted they were using AI to replace workers. Fully 60 percent described their organization as using the technology as a platform to assist the workforce.[3] Process automation will replace some jobs and humans will be augmented by automation to create more value. Moreover, this support should liberate the mind for greater work. Research in this field supports Kingdon's belief, as short-term unemployment driven by automation is expected to be significantly offset by the job creation enabled by upmarket thinking and automation.[4] People will not become less important in work, they will become more important for doing the work that only humans can do, the work that can't be captured or replicated by the logic of the rational brain. People will become important in the workplace (in fact celebrated) for their Intuitive Brain. The brain that leads with emotional caring for others, creates memories for the organizations, and develops shared learning among the organizations cannot be automated.

Empowered with Data

Data is a slightly different, but mostly similar story. A 2018 *Forbes* article demonstrates the true abundance and overwhelming growth of data. With nearly four billion humans on the planet using the internet daily; the proliferation of an internet of things with more devices using the internet; social media that generates more images, sounds, and videos; and digital services we depend on daily, we can expect our data to continue to grow.[5] Large businesses that harness data and leverage it for decision-making will continue to succeed in the economy, while those that struggle with data will likely fail.

However, despite the understanding for the volume and breadth of data, many organizations struggle with how to use the data. Leaders feel challenged to make decisions based on the data in front of them instead of based on "years of expertise". Like Grady in our opening story from the film *Moneyball*, many leaders feel that their industry doesn't work based on data. It works on feel, instinct, gut. The question is – why is it one or the other?

In so many organizations, data volume is high and understanding of data is low. It will be a long time before anyone will trust data alone to make decisions. However, data-informed decisions with data-informed leaders can start now. Thomas Davenport offers practical advice for leaders looking to bridge the gap. He notes that leaders can make themselves the consumers of data, learn a little about analytics, ask hard questions, and create an inquisitive culture that will support data-informed decisions in an organization without data being the sole driver of decisions. In this way, data and people will work together to answer organizational questions.[6]

Unsticking Technology

Many leading organizations will feel an imperative to invest in digital transformation, automation, and data. There really isn't a choice for the elite companies anymore. The question is not when humans will get on board with the technologies, but how. Our lessons in attachment become instructive in helping us work through these cases.

Experience the Change. We know that attachment emerges in the Limbic System where memory, emotions, and learning come together. This means that effective change is better experienced that discussed. The conversation alone will lead the individual to go to their own memories of similar experiences and the associated emotions. To re-shape those memories around new technology, leaders must help users experience the change that is coming. With most technology solutions, this means giving them a demo or prototype that that can see. The more tailored, the better.

The more advanced, the better. The more the user can see themselves and their work in the solution, the more likely they are to be willing to use the solution for their own work – the more likely they will adopt.

Live in the Transition. In all three of these cases, there is a transitional period from the mostly human way of living to the mostly technology-driven future we believe is coming. As a result, we are clearly in a transitional space with relation to technology. While we emphasized the importance of the transitional space for driving change, it is also a critical place for creativity and PLAY. Leaders should encourage their teams to be creative with new technology solutions, to PLAY with new tools, and develop innovative solutions that yield new value for the organization. Practically, this means creating opportunities for co-creation and solution-making among team members with new platforms and technology to encourage PLAY as a way of engagement.

Tech Serves Us. Since technology serves humans and not the other way around, the messaging of technological transformation needs to remind people how technology serves them – how will it make their lives easier. To play on the old familiar quote from President Kennedy, leaders need to "Ask not what employees will do for technology, but what technology will do for the team." A simple turn of phrase that will remind the organization where the priorities reside. Moreover, technology should create connection and bring disparate groups of the organization together to collaborate. It should not create haves and have-nots or differences among the organization.

Evolve Tech Emotionally, Not Necessarily Logically. Organizations must move slowly through new technology adoption up a maturity curve from a known current emotional state through a transition space to a Future State. Trying to jump people from the known emotional present to the unknown with illogical leaps can hurt the brain and will only yield resistance. Bitcoin, social media, and privacy all demonstrate the same lesson here. On Bitcoin, many Americans do not touch paper money daily, so why are younger people more likely to adopt bitcoin? Because they grew up in a world of not touching paper money. They have memories of money that is almost entirely connected to an electronic platform.

As a result, the mental leap to an algorithm as the basic trust mechanism and backing for the currency is not a difficult logical leap. The same is true with each progressive social media platform – when you are familiar with sharing a story, a picture makes sense, and then a video. And while some are greatly concerned with privacy, others freely give the privacy away in exchange for both access to content and the valued social clout. The brain makes the journey and if the brain has the memories, emotions, and learning that support the logical next step in advancement then it is easier to make that step. If not, then an easier former object may be the safer place for the brain to attach.

OUR EVOLVING WORKFORCE

As we concluded in our discussion on technology in the workplace, it is not about technology, but about people. We need to make our organizations more human. So, what's happening with people? Quite a lot! We have five generations working simultaneously, we have just had a global pandemic, there is a global crisis of burnout, and there are social issues that previously quiet companies must address. Our workforce is changing and evolving against the backdrop of efficiency pressures that emerge from the technology fallacy. Due to this trend, too many leaders believe that investments in technology should yield immediate efficiency outcomes. The result is that people need to make up the gap by stretching and overworking. What happens when one more change comes along? Is our brain ready for it? Nope. It's Stuck.

The Generational Gaps

Over the last decade, the American workforce has been undergoing a significant evolution. It started with the Great Financial Crisis. As a result of losses in the housing and financial markets, many Baby Boomers (and some in the Silent Generation) generation decided to delay retirement. Next, the oversized Millennial generation started to move up the ranks in organizations and become leaders across industries. Third, Generation Z started to join the workforce *en masse*. These trends have collectively led to five generations in the workforce and five generations governing wealth. For example, there is a 72-year age gap between the world's oldest working billionaire (Warren Buffett) and the youngest working billionaire (Kevin David Lehmann).

This age range in the workforce creates a shift in expectations. In their 80-year review of the Gallup workforce data, Jim Clifton and Jim Harter found a marked shift in the way workers are thinking about their roles. People continue to move away from an emphasis on their paycheck to an emphasis on purpose, from a desire for simple satisfaction to continued development, and from simply a job to a holistic view of their life. The impact on organizations is that they: cannot provide a boss, but rather a coach; should not provide a point-in-time annual review, but an ongoing review about performance; and can't just critique, but really need to develop strengths. If this all sounds a little Pollyannaish; it's not meant to be. There is real accountability in everything written here, but these attributes are necessary to attract and retain the attention of talent.[7]

The attention of talent is purposeful phrasing because it is not just employment anymore. In the gig economy, employers need to retain the full attention of employees. Prior to the pandemic, it is estimated that 36 percent of Americans were engaging in gigs, whether these were their primary role or not.[8] We often hear the phrase, "There is no loyalty today." That's an easy quip to use, but what came first – the employees' departure or the organizational pullback in incentives? Well, arguably organizations changed behavior first. With decreases in pensions, then a decrease in 401(k) contributions, then a move to high-deductible insurance, and changes in other benefits; the burden for self-care and long-term self-reliance continues to shift more and more to the employee. What is the incentive for loyalty?

We think there is something that attachment can offer as a bridge for organizations to create loyalty and support employees the way they need to be supported. With so many generations in the workforce at the same time, we know that there is likely to be generational and work-life blurring. Let's take a 50-year-old man who is working in your average Fortune 50 professional services organization. He is well-educated with a living father and two children who have both recently finished college.

In his role, at work, it is possible he may observe employees who start to look like his children and superiors who look like his father. It is hard enough for him to manage the stress of balancing the multiple roles at work and at home. Now, he must think about balancing his emotional barriers to treat these groups differently. Could he slip and treat an employee with the same candor he might one of her children? Could he lose patience with his father and bring that to a superior at work? Of course, and no one could fault him. Because, as we learned in Chapter 2, the Intuitive Brain is seeking analogues or mental models to make our life easier. Sometimes, these emotions can be misaligned to the people and situations around us.

Organizations can help in this process by re-thinking developmental paths for people at different points of their career. First, organizations can create roles that simply reduce stress and the level of engagement for those being squeezed by parenthood and parents at the same time. This is a practical matter. Second, there can be a conscious decoupling of the emotional tracks that are likely to lead to unhealthy analogues, such as parent-child mentorship relationships. Another way of discovering these challenges is through something like the Attachment Styles Index with the LMX (Chapter 8), where leaders can identify how to best align with followers. Third, there is a need to continue to educate workers on their emotional needs in the workplace and how to develop emotional awareness. Often branded as wellness programs, these solutions provide a better connection between employees and the Intuitive Brain that makes them more creative thinkers, more efficient employees, and more effective leaders.

Covid and the Workplace of the Future

The global impact of Covid-19 is still stunning. The entire situation has created uncertainty, confusion, and loss. Many struggle with health issues and the unimaginable loss of loved ones. Others have suffered the loss of their previously secure workplace swiftly disappearing into thin air. Over 48 million American workers were suddenly forced to work from home, and these were the lucky ones. All these situations created a sense of loss. At the time this book is being finished, it is an open question whether the post-pandemic workplace will "return to normal." Most articles suggest it will not. And they are probably right.

Prior to the Covid-19 pandemic, only seven percent of workers in the United States had a flexible workplace benefit or telework. However, the trend toward remote work was on the rise with the remote workforce growing by 159 percent between 2005 and 2017.[9] During the height of the pandemic a staggering 42 percent of the total U.S. workforce was working from home full-time.[10] Many workers asked to maintain the role of remote worker in a post-pandemic period. Many employers looking to reduce their facility footprint would be content to oblige. The question we pose is – what is the organizational implication of such a decision?

First, there is the challenge of culture. Whether it is culture creation, acculturation, or culture maintenance; there is no doubt that it is harder to build and sustain a culture in a remote setting. As we noted previously, culture is the unseen not the visible, so building that unseen behavior can be even harder when it cannot be casually observed. Additionally, we have emphasized the importance of emotion and memory. Despite some wonderful efforts, memories developed on screen are simply not the same as memories developed in-person. The shared emotion is not the same and it leads to culture and behavior being stored differently by our brains. A memory is combination of the full sensory experience held together – time, place, people, sight, sound, smell, and conversation. If many of these elements are the same as in your home except for the person's face on screen and the conversation, how do you create the same kind of shared memory? How do you create an organizational culture?

Second, there is the issue of teaching new employees. While many current employees adapted well during the pandemic (many, not all); organizational thinking about a long-term remote workforce will need to solve for onboarding remotely. This is a different challenge. Much of our service and knowledge economy depends on learning through an apprenticeship model that is not easy to replicate remotely. In fact, it may be impossible to replicate remotely. Casual questions get lost, there is no watercooler, and there is no "learning by osmosis" that happens from the casually overheard conversation. The absence of learning that happens in a shared space will be a challenge for many to overcome.

Third, there is the issue of work-life balance. We still do not know which way this balance goes in the post-covid world. Some have suggested that productivity increased for those working from home during the pandemic; others have said they felt more stress at home. Some said they were able to have more balance. The truth is we just don't know yet how this impacts us. But we do know from attachment studies that there is an important transition period in all things and that working from home does remove that transition between two important parts of our life. What many people dismiss as the commute is a downtime to separate work from the rest of life and for many people it is necessary to stop thinking about their work and be ready to engage with the rest of their life. What happens when the rest of their life is one room (or just 10 feet) away?

Many articles agree that the most likely workplace of the future will be a hybrid work environment. This will lead to more time at home for those who want it with available workspace for those seeking the space. Given what we have discussed in this book about attachment styles, we know some will seek the space based on their need for social attachments. Given what we have written about culture, certain organizations will breed a desirable space for people to come and work. Given what we know about attachment in general, we believe that most will learn more effectively in-person. But all of this will have to play out over the next years or decades as we all form new ways of working and learning together in our new less formal normal.

Battling Burnout

Covid also exacerbated an organizational challenge that was already brewing – burnout. In 2003 the National Library of Medicine indexed 307 articles with the term "burnout," which grew to 560 articles in 2009 and 2,137 articles in 2019.[11] In 2019, the World Health Organization (WHO) classified burnout as a disease and in 2022 will refer to burnout as an occupational syndrome. Even prior to the pandemic some of the worst symptoms of burnout were in the health care industry, where long shifts were the norm of upcoming residents. Stephen Trzeciak found that burnout among doctors not only leads to a decline in good decision-making, but a decline in compassion for patients.[12]

Moreover, there is a real financial cost to burnout. As employees struggle, they disengage, which leads to a reduction in value for their salary of an average of 34 percent. Furthermore, as many as half of these employees will attrit, which has an additional cost in replacement of labor. There is also the healthcare cost, which is estimated between $125 and $190 billion a year in the United States alone.[13]

Covid made this all worse. According to a KPMG survey of CIOs, 84 percent of leaders within organizations reported they were concerned with the mental health of their team due to the circumstances of the pandemic.[14] With good reason! During the pandemic, 89 percent of respondents to one survey noted their work life "was getting worse" and 85 percent said their well-being has declined.[15]

So what's to be done? Victoria has been working with DHG Healthcare People and Change Team to focus research and attention on this issue in the workplace. Over the last year, they have published a series of articles to shed some light on the challenges of burnout in the healthcare industry and beyond.[16]

The first step is to acknowledge burnout is an *organizational* issue. Despite the WHO declaration, many organizational leaders still view burnout as a personal problem. Yet, nothing could be further from the truth. As we have seen throughout our discussions in this book, organizations intentionally build attachments with their employees via culture, training, communications, and employee agreements. We have also seen that the employment relationship is a relationship between the organization, the leader, and the employee. The organization must take its part in the relationship. Research identifies six main causes of burnout:

- Unsustainable workload
- Perceived lack of control
- Insufficient rewards for effort
- Lack of a supportive community
- Lack of fairness
- Mismatched values and skills

Of these six areas, all of them have an *opportunity* for organizational systems to support employees. Please note, the language is opportunity, not obligation.

Second, organizations need to dig into their data to understand the challenges of their own people. Broad perspectives on the economy may not apply to every organization. It is critical that leaders understand what is happening in their organization for their people. A survey on burnout is also an excellent opportunity to explore some of the other underlying relationships in the organization, such as the Attachment Styles Index, Change Diagnostic Index, or the Culture Study. The most important may be understanding the Leader-Follower relationships with the Attachment Styles Index. Often direct supervisor behavior, or simply a disconnect with an employee, can be an unintended consequence of organizational systems.

Third, build a roadmap to "bend the curve." Assuming that the organization is , like all others, facing the burnout challenge today, then there is an opportunity to develop tangible next steps to support people through their burnout. Just like other changes, the plan would include active re-training of the Intuitive Brain to drive new behavior through effective communications, possibly some experiential training, and strong performance management to test progress against stated behavioral change. Through these steps, an organization can build the right path to battling burnout.

Discussing Diversity

The last few years have not just been challenging due to Covid. They also included the racial tension in the United States, and globally, sparked by the murder of George Floyd. The Black Lives Matter movement has again moved the ever-present challenge of race in America to the foreground of conversation. The conversation, the protests, and the tension with police created a necessary reckoning in many businesses about their own diversity and inclusion policies. Many organizations opted to go beyond the stance for a diverse workforce toward an anti-racist society.

The decision to support Black Lives Matter, to become an anti-racist organization, or to support a host of other social activist policies requires its own organizational reckoning. We have been working with Tyece Wilkins to explore the connection between these corporate decisions on the Black Lives Matter movement and attachment. Wilkins discovered a powerful link between the two. She noticed that often employees believe a new conversation around race is akin to breaking the psychological contract we discussed in Chapter 5. However, this may be a necessary break to advance the organization toward new social objectives the leadership wants to pursue.

First, we know that discussions of race elicit emotional responses. As a result, many organizations avoid the conversation altogether. However, we also know that this emotional response means the reaction resides in the Limbic System and is part of the Intuitive Brain. That means we are likely dealing with an attachment. Organizations need to welcome the conversation.

Second, organizations need to consider bringing in external facilitators to drive the organizational conversations on race. These conversations require psychological safety and expertise with the subject matter, one wrong move can cause the conversation to go sideways. Worse than that, one wrong move from an executive can cause others to lose respect for the entire process. Third, since we know this topic hits on attachments, we need to dig deeper, to dig past the initial layer of attachments and mental models to an additional layer of mentals models where common ground can be found. Perhaps that next level is an attachment to the organization, perhaps it is an attachment to a religion or the nation.

Fourth, organizations need to support helping some individuals who have the right connective stories to become allies of the racial equality movement. These change agents can become transitional objects in the process of supporting change within the organization. A business may even consider training individuals to develop a well-rounded story that will resonate with more people across the organization. Last, companies need to be intentional about how to position their mission toward social issues. Each organization can find meaningful ways to authentically support social objectives, but the key is to have authentic alignment of social and financial objectives. A business that lacks the right social aims for their lines of business will likely suffer criticism and reputational issues in the market.

WHAT DOES IT ALL MEAN?

We're Stuck, but we don't have to be. The purpose of this book was to bring together the lessons of research on the brain and attachment to help you understand how you can help yourself (as an individual and leader) and your organization. To that end, here are the top five lessons we think you should take away from this book for individuals, for leaders, and for organizations:

Five Key Takeaways for Individuals

1. I create attachments through memory, learning, and emotion. These are good and help me connect with the people and places around me. (Chapters 2 and 3)
2. When I lose something (whether is tangible or abstract) it may cause a sense of loss. That is okay and normal. The important thing is how I regulate myself through that experience. (Chapter 3)
3. I have an attachment style that is based on the unique experiences of my life; this likely informs who I am, how I interact with others, how I interact with my work environment, and I how respond to the sense of loss. (Chapter 4)

4. Certain objects help me through this sense of loss. I want to identify the right objects for me, so that I can feel more comfortable with the transition and move through the situation securely. (Chapter 5)
5. During times of change, all these feelings become more intense. Even small changes may make me feel like I am losing something big. I need to identify what I may be losing, understand my emotions, and identify the objects (people, places, or ideas) that will help me through the change. (Chapter 7)

Five Key Takeaways for Leaders

1. When I lose something (whether is tangible or abstract) it may cause a sense of loss. That is okay and normal. The important thing is how I regulate myself through that experience *and how well I demonstrate that regulation to others*. (Chapters 3 and 8)
2. I have an attachment style that is based on the unique experiences of my life, and it may not resonate with my followers. I need to consider how to manage my attachment style based on my followers and the situation we face. (Chapters 4 and 8)
3. I need to connect with my own emotions to help my team connect with their emotions. This will help me construct shared experiences for my team and build the right visuals or stories to communicate how we will collectively address challenges as a group. (Chapter 8)
4. I need to develop transitional objects when we are going through a change that will help our team move from the Current State to a Future State...and acknowledge I might be one of them. (Chapters 5 and 8)
5. I need to set the stage with the connection to our mission then encourage different types of communication (visual and verbal), different types of collaboration (virtual and in-person), different types of co-creation (playful and formal), and diverse thinking to speak to our broad workforce and the challenges ahead. (Chapters 7, 8 and 9)

Five Key Takeaways for Organizations

1. Leverage unique assessments that account for the lessons of attachment including the Attachment Styles Index, the Change Diagnostic Index, and the Culture Study. (Chapters 4, 6, and 7)

2. Build a culture that connects employees to a purpose and allows them to build their own attachments to the organization while supporting the overall mission of the organization. (Chapters 6 and 7)
3. Develop leaders that understand the importance of attachment among their team members, can identify their own attachment style, and can communicate their own role during a change. (Chapters 4, 6, 7, and 8)
4. Plan for change by building the capability to change – re-think training, communications, and performance management – and aligning transitional objects to support your people through the many changes ahead. (Chapter 8)
5. Own the future by organizing around the way the brain works now to account for shifts in demographics, expectations, and economic trends that will change the workplace tomorrow. (Chapters 8 and 9)

Attachment behavior is an instinctual response that begins in our earliest days of life and impacts how we connect and interact with the world around us. Attachment can be positive. It can create strong cohesion among workers, help build a productive culture, and make people excited to come to work. When those objects are taken away or are no longer available, then people can feel a real and acute sense of loss. This loss can profoundly impact the ability of the individuals to complete daily work tasks and impact the productivity of organizations.

Understanding attachment is a powerful tool for leaders and organizations. It can help us create the right kind of work environment for our employees, create an effective culture, and create a Stickiness within the organization. We do this with a combination of memory, emotions, and learning via the brain that combines with the positive experiences our employees have from the past. The trick is to create a Stickiness without letting employees become Stuck. We know the only certainty is that we will change some aspect of the organization they have come to appreciate.

We are all on a journey. Whether it is a new strategy, a new leader, a new process, or new technology; something will cause a shift in the workplace that will make us change. And when it happens, we need to take the time to remember that we helped the brain attach to the previous strategy, leader, process, or technology, and now we need to help undo it. We need to help it become Unstuck. We also need to remember that on this journey is our human brain that developed just a few thousand years ago. Unlike our advances in technology, it does not develop on Moore's law. The brain evolves more slowly, more generationally, perhaps even glacially. We must remember that on this journey, our society is the hare blasting forward, but our brain is the tortoise still plodding along. We may want to run with the hare, but when leading organizations, we move with the tortoise. Our leaders, our people, and our brains are all necessary for the journey. Are we ready? Or are we likely to get Stuck?

PRACTICAL EXERCISES

 COLLECT: CONNECTING WITH TECHNOLOGY

As we discussed above, technology can have a very strong role in supporting connectivity and it can have a role in creating silos. Too often, as new technologies are deployed, people feel the disconnection before the connection. The purpose of this exercise is to find the connection in the technology. This exercise can easily be done as a group exercise.

1. Think of a technology in the organization.
2. Describe/write-down the purpose of the technology.
3. Now, describe/write-down how the organization would complete that same purpose without the technology.
4. Think about the following questions:
   o Would there be more or less communication without the technology?
      - If more, why?
      - If less, why?
   o Would more communication be a good thing for this process or a bad thing?
      - If good, how could the current technology increase communication?
      - If bad, how could the current technology decrease communication?
   o Does the technology make you do more work than you would have to do without it?

- If yes, is there a logical reason for this?
- If no, good.
  ○ Do you remember how this technology was introduced to you?
    - How did you feel about it at the time?
    - How do you feel about it now?
      - If it changed at all, what caused it to change?
      - If it is the same, what might cause that to change?

 REFLECT: LOSS IN THE TIME OF COVID-19

Covid-19 has been a difficult time for many people around the world. We sincerely hope that no one experienced the loss of loved ones during this period or personally struggled with the disease. We also hope that no one struggled with any of the difficulty of depression that many people felt during this period. There were undoubtedly some lesser losses that you felt daily that impacted your life and your work. The purpose of this exercise is to think about those areas and think about how they impacted each other.

1. List out some of the changes in your life due to Covid-19.
2. Circle the changes that you would think of as losses.
3. Look at the things you did not circle; should you re-write them to sound more like losses?
4. Label the losses as either "work" or "life."
5. Looking at the list, take the three top "work" losses and list them on the right-hand side of a page.
6. List the top three "life" losses on the left-hand side of the same page.
7. Answer the following questions:
   ○ Are these losses related?
   ○ Is there any way that the "work" losses support the "life" losses?
   ○ Do the "life" losses help the "work" losses?
   ○ Is there any sort of transitional object you think you created for yourself during this period? If so, what? Did you create it for just yourself or others, too?

8. Write the transitional objects between the two lists of "work" losses and "life" losses. Could you use this transitional object again?

9. As you think about the post-pandemic world, what things will change back on this list? What will stay the same?

10. Most importantly, what do you have control of to change back the way you want and what will remain the same based on the decisions of your organization or others in your life?

 REFLECT AND APPLY: BURNOUT ASSESSMENT

According to Christina Maslach of the University of California, Berkeley, Susan E. Jackson of Rutgers, and Michael Leiter of Deakin University, burnout has six main causes. As we mentioned above, these causes have an opportunity for organizations to build systems to support employees feeling burnout.

• When you think about your own work situation, do you think you are burning out?
  ○ If so, which of the following causes is contributing to your burnout?
  ○ If not, which of the following causes is likely to cause you to burn out in your organization?

Circle the cause or causes (or likely cause or causes) below:
  – Unsustainable workload
  – Perceived lack of control
  – Insufficient rewards for effort
  – Lack of a supportive community
  – Lack of fairness
  – Mismatched values and skills

• As we learned in Chapter 8, leadership can have a lot to do with the direct feelings of an employee. When you think about your feelings, do you think that the cause is a result of your work situation, your supervisor, or a result of the organizational systems in place? Table 9.1 provides an opportunity for you to fill and track which applies to you. Put an X in the box for the possible sources.

TABLE 9.1

Burnout Self-Assessment

	Your Situation	Supervisor Behavior	Organizational Systems
Unsustainable workload			
Perceived lack of control			
Insufficient rewards for effort			
Lack of a supportive community			
Lack of fairness			
Mismatched values and skills			

- Now, thinking about how to solve the challenges of burnout for you, do you think the solution for your cause will come from a change in your situation, your supervisor's behavior, or organizational systems? Put a check mark in the box that applies.
- What would be that possible solution? How feasible is that? What would need to happen for that solution to be realized?

 APPLY: BUILDING NEW PSYCHOLOGICAL CONTRACTS

Your organization may need to break existing psychological contracts to develop new approaches to diversity or social issues. It is important to identify the existing psychological contract and what is fundamentally changing in the organization for the employees (if anything) to write the new psychological contract. Table 9.2 is a template for this process:

It is important to note, that during the process, it is possible that employees may find very littles is changing for *most* people. There could be a vocal minority that is clinging to a mythological past that is no longer present in the organization. This exercise can highlight that difference among employees.

TABLE 9.2

Building a New Psychological Contract

	Old Contract	New Contract
The primary role of employees is to…		
The primary role of managers is to…		
Employees who perform well will…		
Employees who do not perform well will…		
The primary source of development is…		
Employees are expected to stay for…		

NOTES

1 Kane, G. (2019). "The Technology Fallacy." *Research-Technology Management, 62*(6), pp. 44–49.
2 Roose, K. (2021). "The Robots are Coming for Phil in Accounting." *The New York Times*. Accessed electronically on July 3, 2021 at: www.nytimes.com/2021/03/06/business/the-robots-are-coming-for-phil-in-accounting.html
3 Deloitte Insights. (2020.) "The Social Enterprise at Work: Paradox As a Path Forward." 2020 Deloitte Global Human Capital Trends Survey, Accessed electronically on July 3, 2021 at: www2.deloitte.com/cn/en/pages/human-capital/articles/global-human-capital-trends-2020.html, p. 54.
4 Mincer, J. and Danninger, S. (2000). "Technology, Unemployment, and Inflation." National Bureau of Economic Research Working Paper No. w7817.
5 Marr, B. (2018). "How Much Data Do We Create Every Day? The Mind-Blowing Stats Everyone Should Read." *Forbes*. May 21, 2018. Accessed electronically on July 3, 2021 at: www.forbes.com/sites/bernardmarr/2018/05/21/how-much-data-do-we-create-every-day-the-mind-blowing-stats-everyone-should-read/?sh=27dc71b160ba.
6 Davenport, T. (2013). "Keep Up with Your Quants." *Harvard Business Review*. July-August. Accessed electronically on July 3, 2021 at: https://hbr.org/2013/07/keep-up-with-your-quants.
7 Clifton, J. and Harter, J. (2019). *It's the Manager*. New York: Gallup Press.
8 Abraham, K., Haltiwanger, J., Sandusky, K., and Spletzer, J. (2018.) "Measuring the Gig Economy: Current Knowledge and Open Issues." National Bureau of Economic Research Working Paper No. 24950. Accessed electronically on July 3, 2021 at: www.nber.org/system/files/working_papers/w24950/w24950.pdf.
9 Valet, V. (2020). "Working From Home During The Coronavirus Pandemic: What You Need To Know." *Forbes*. March 12, 2020. Accessed electronically on July 3, 2021 at: www.forbes.com/sites/vickyvalet/2020/03/12/working-from-home-during-the-coronavirus-pandemic-what-you-need-to-know/?sh=3162213f1421.

10 Wong, M. (2020). "Stanford Research Provides a Snapshot of a New Working-from-Home Economy." *Stanford News*. Accessed electronically on July 3, 2021 at: https://news.stanford.edu/2020/06/29/snapshot-new-working-home-economy/.

11 Marchalik, D. (2020). "What Health Care Can Teach Other Industries About Preventing Burnout." *Harvard Business Review Online*. October 26, 2020. Accessed electronically on July 3, 2021 at: https://hbr.org/2020/10/what-health-care-can-teach-other-industries-about-preventing-burnout.

12 Trzeciak, S. (2018). "Healthcare's Compassion Crisis." TED Talk. April 2018. Accessed electronically on July 3, 2021 at: www.ted.com/talks/stephen_trzeciak_healthcare_s_compassion_crisis_jan_2018.

13 Blanding, M. (2015). "National Health Costs Could Decrease if Managers Reduce Work Stress." *Harvard Business School Working Knowledge*. January 26, 2015. As accessed electronically on July 3, 2021 at: https://hbswk.hbs.edu/item/national-health-costs-could-decrease-if-managers-reduce-work-stress.

14 Harvey Nash and KPMG. (2020). CIO Survey 2020. Accessed electronically on July 3, 2021 at: https://assets.kpmg/content/dam/kpmg/xx/pdf/2020/10/harvey-nash-kpmg-cio-survey-2020.pdf, p. 28.

15 Moss, J. (2021). "Beyond Burned Out." *Harvard Business Review: Big Idea Series*. February 10, 2021. Accessed electronically on July 3, 2021 at: https://hbr.org/2021/02/beyond-burned-out.

16 Grady, V., Rich, C., and Spohn, S. (2021). "Putting Out the Fire: What Causes Organizational
    'Burnout' and How to Fix It." DHG Perspectives. March 2021. Accessed electronically on July 3, 2021 at:www.dhg.com/Portals/0/ResourceMedia/publications/Burnout-Mindset-Shift-and-Steps-Forward-DHG-Healthcare.pdf?ver=2021-03-16-0630 47-400.

    Grady, V., Rich, C., and Spohn, S. (2021.) "Burnout: What It Is, Isn't, and Your Role." DHG Perspectives. April 2021. Accessed electronically on July 3, 2021 at: www.dhg.com/Portals/0/ResourceMedia/publications/Burnout-What-it-is-isnt-and-your-role.pdf?ver=2021-04-07-083740-553.

Index

Printed in the United States
by Baker & Taylor Publisher Services